D1367668

Building Babies Better

Developing a Solid Foundation for Your Child

Second Edition

Roxanne Small, PT

Order this book online at www.trafford.com
or email orders@trafford.com

Most Trafford titles are also available at major online book retailers.

The stories in this book are real life events. The names of the children have been changed to protect their
privacy. This book is designed to present concepts and information to parents of young children. It is
not meant to be used in place of therapy or any other professional services.

Printed in the United States of America.

ISBN: 978-1-4669-1455-1 (sc)
ISBN: 978-1-4669-1456-8 (hc)
ISBN: 978-1-4669-1457-5 (e)

Library of Congress Control Number: 2012902717

Trafford rev. 03/22/2012

 www.trafford.com

North America & international
toll-free: 1 888 232 4444 (USA & Canada)
phone: 250 383 6864 ♦ fax: 812 355 4082

This book is dedicated to
Alicia, Blake, Tyler and their future babies.

To God be the Glory...
the ultimate builder of all babies!

Acknowledgments

A journey starts with a single step, and certainly that single step for *Building Babies Better* started with Ed Snapp, PT. His genius and insight have inspired many and he is greatly missed. During his time with us he shared his visions with some, taught many his concepts behind Chronologically Controlled Developmental Therapy, and most importantly helped thousands of children and adults build a more solid sensory-motor foundation so that their level of function improved dramatically. There are no words to acknowledge his importance to this work.

As in the first edition, I have had a team of people who taught me, supported me and encouraged me. Julie Erbaugh, PT is my teaching partner extraordinaire! You cannot do a journey alone and I can't think of anyone I would rather have to walk beside me. You will hear more about Dinah Reilly, PT, PhD, but her input into this edition was invaluable. Susan Crowe, PT and Marcia Graham OTR spent countless hours in edits and conversations. Bev Sector, OTR and Renee Malina were instrumental in getting the original project off the ground. Amy Butcher designed the cover and played a key role in the first edition. Added to this spectacular team are the many therapists, parents, and children who have shared time with me along the way. It is pure joy to work with a baby and their family. My husband is the last to receive acknowledgement, but offered the most to this team. Without his support and encouragement, I would have never started the journey.

Preface

When *Building Babies Better* was first published in 2005, the goal was simply to get people thinking about the impact activities we were using on young babies had on development. Some of the ideas I presented in the book were a bit radical for the time, but overall the ideas and activities were ones that many in my field recommended. The problem was good sensory motor activities for babies were not being taught to parents. I heard and was part of many discussions with professionals, but found a void in the knowledge most parents had in this area.

In the past 6 years I have had opportunities to discuss my book with people all over the country and some in other countries. I have taught many seminars on these concepts. Almost everyone has responded with the same enthusiasm that I have and they ask my same questions . . . why isn't this being taught more, written about more, and shouted from the roof tops? These are our precious children we are talking about and these concepts and recommendations are not difficult to understand or follow. I have waited with anticipation for signs that many others were going to help teach and write on these very important subjects. And a few have . . . too few. I have waited with anticipation for the number of children using "containers" to lessen . . . and the opposite has happened. According to statistics on the number of current children experiencing plagiocephaly (misshapen skull) the problem has increased. I have waited for pediatricians to advertise their "Back to Sleep Tummy to Play" campaign with the same vigor as they did in 1992 when they first promoted their "Back to Sleep" campaign . . . I am still waiting.

On a positive note, *Building Babies Better* has gone places I never dreamed possible. Hospitals are using this book for parenting classes, missionaries have taken it to Africa, it has been a source of great discussions at baby showers, and some day care centers have radically changed their environments because of it. I have been encouraged by parents and professionals to continue on in this effort to improve the lives of our children. Some have joined me in teaching these concepts, and for that I am grateful.

I have appreciated those who were brave enough and took the time to offer truthful criticism. In this category I heard often that there was no bibliography and they questioned if there was scientific evidence to support the concepts. I agreed with this criticism. This is the reason I have done a revision of *Building Babies Better.* For the past two and a half years I have immersed myself in reading research. I owe a great deal of gratitude to my colleague and friend, Dinah Reilly, PT, PhD. She started me on this journey of becoming enthused about research! She patiently discussed articles, pointed me in the direction of good research and showed me how to better understand the findings. I will tell you that reading research for some of us is addicting!! Thanks for this addiction Dinah! I struggled with how to communicate this research. One of the aspects of the book many said they enjoyed was it was a quick read. My main target audience is parents and they certainly do not have extra time. Therefore I have decided to put a bibliography at the end of the book that is organized by chapters. In parentheses after each listing I summarize my personal thoughts about the research or article or in some cases put in quotes some statements that were meaningful to me. In this way I hope it will be usable to those who would like to look a bit deeper at a certain recommendation. The very best would be if you would look up the research and read it for yourself, coming to your own conclusions. Watch out, it may be addicting!

Table of Contents

Part III

Introduction

Anticipation and Preparation

The moment a couple realizes they are going to be parents is a moment utterly consumed with anticipation. Visions of the days, weeks, and months ahead fill the mind. If they are like most, they dream of what their child will look like, what gifts their child will have and what they will accomplish. Above all else, the dreams include their child growing into a strong, bright and happy adult. When parents hold a precious newborn in their arms, they are eager to provide an environment that will allow their child to grow into a child who can weather the storms of life. As noble as these intentions may be, what are the tools that are needed to accomplish this lofty mission? Society tells new parents they will need an endless supply of baby equipment, toys, and educational tools to give their child every advantage for a bright future. It is not uncommon for expectant parents to have a baby store registry list that rivals the one they had for their wedding. But is this necessary? A better question is, will all these items help or hinder? Anticipation turns into the need for preparation.

Often, preparation requires a serious look at how others have prepared. For a new parent, there is no shortage of people offering advice! In addition to this, there is a plethora of parenting books and stores filled with baby items. There is so much information it is important to find a way to evaluate what is worthwhile and what is not. This evaluation requires a parent to understand for what they are preparing their child. What is the goal? Too many recommendations and far too much equipment prepare babies to look smarter, push their development faster, and be visually entertained. After all, the world we are giving this child is one that is moving fast and is filled with technology. There is some logic in starting early. But is this the best preparation? With childhood obesity, attention deficit disorders, autism, and mental illness related problems on the rise, it should cause a parent to question the preparations they will choose for their child. Remember the goal: raising a child who will grow into a well-balanced adult. The goal is not raising a child who is the first to achieve their developmental milestones. These two goals require very different preparations.

Building Babies Better is one tool parents can use to prepare for the goal of raising a child who is strong and happy, a child who will be a well balanced adult. This book is designed to encourage parents of infants and toddlers to focus their attention on the physical aspect of their child's foundational years. Children who have a more solid base of sensory-motor development have an easier time handling stress. Picture a child's development as a structure, a pyramid-like structure. The broader the foundation of that pyramid, the less chance it will have of toppling over. The sturdier the foundation, the more weight it can support. Think of the blocks in the foundation of a child's development as starting out empty and hollow. As the child grows and matures, many of those blocks become filled with experiences. One of the goals of this book is to increase parents' confidence by giving them key principles to use in choosing experiences and environments that will provide their children with a strong sensory-motor foundation.

Before you go further, you may be asking yourself why you might read this book to prepare for your child's development rather than many of the other books available. After all, there are so many theories about development. Although no one fully understands how the brain works and how we can impact brain development, experience is a great teacher. This book is built on my 35 years working as a pediatric physical therapist alongside some of the finest professionals available. Couple that with an extensive study of research and an openness to understand various approaches to development, and *Building Babies Better* is built on a solid foundation itself! Not only are the concepts presented solid, but the recommendations are time tested. Every recommendation in this book has been put into practice for almost 30 years. I have the amazing experience of being a mother of three children. I have personally used all of these recommendations with either my own children or the children I work with professionally. At the end of this book I have chapters addressing special needs children and bonding with adoptive children. Two of our children entered our family through adoption, so again I am speaking from experience. This second edition has the advantage of input from thousands of parents and professionals who read the first edition. Here are some of their comments:

"This book is key to our ability to get control of the growing numbers of children with learning disabilities, attention difficulties, and developmental delays."

"This book provides basic, practical ideas for every parent."

"I feel as though this book helps parents to focus on the basic building blocks (note the title) to healthy development, as opposed to stressing out because your child in not meeting certain milestones. The "back to basics" ideas really make sense. The book is extremely easy to follow, and there are real life illustrations of the techniques. I feel as though that being able to physically participate in my child's development truly empowers me as a parent."

"We LOVE this book. We have already used the massage and movement techniques suggested in the book with our 4 month old. He started scooting on his belly last week because of the slick plastic and oil she suggests in the book. This has developed the right muscles for him to start to move. He LOVES the massage and it calms him down during the day and before he goes to sleep at night. I wished I had this book while I was pregnant with him. I would not have registered for 1/2 of the stuff that I did. I loved how she explains the needs of each stage. This book is a REALLY easy and quick read. I hope more parents read this book. I found the book to help simplify our lives instead of feeling like we needed a million developmental toys for our baby!"

A final note on parents' choices for preparing their child's environment for good development: one of the aspects I believe very strongly in is the concept of making choices that have a positive long term impact on a child. I have watched as far too many choices are made for children based on the immediate time frame. These choices include activities that will pacify baby, choices that will make a child talk earlier or choices that will push a child ahead with developmental milestones. These choices look at making the child easier to handle or appear brighter at this developmental stage, but some of the choices could have a negative impact on the long term development of the child. It is interesting to note that research has not been done on the long term impacts of much of our current child rearing practices including the equipment we are using. Understandably it is a difficult task. For example, in the field of physical therapy, often the end result for the success of a child's physical development is thought to be the ability to walk. Research is just beginning to understand the complexities and multi-dimensional aspects of the effects of sensory-motor development on every other area of development such as speech, mental ability, and emotional maturity. It is no longer adequate to find a motor milestone check list and check off as the child passes each step. Quality and endurance of each activity is as important as doing the activity. The exact age these milestones are met is of less importance than we had previously thought. Each child having a variety of options for movement turns out to be a critical factor. This may all seem a bit overwhelming. As parents, it is not necessary to be an expert in development. It *is* important, however, that the parent know enough to make educated choices. Relying on advertising from those interested in selling baby equipment and programs to make babies appear smarter is not good preparation for making these choices. *Building Babies Better* is an excellent start to preparing for all of the decisions parents will make for their child. It is not possible, nor necessary, to know about all areas of development to be a great parent. This book is not meant to be a program that needs to be followed strictly to assure good development. It is my hope that by reading this book and understanding key principles, parents will face their decisions with added confidence and that more babies will have solid sensory-motor foundations to take them into a bright and happy future!

Chapter 1

Sensory-Motor Development

Development is multi-dimensional and complex, occurs in a chronological order, and is built not only from a foundation of genetic information but also from previous, early experiences. The most basic blocks of this foundation are early sensory-motor experiences. Because each experience builds on another, the nervous system can use the information from a previously learned activity for a new activity. When growth occurs in an orderly progression, the new activity is learned more easily and in a more coordinated manner than if a previous step was skipped.

Movement, cognition, and perceptual skills are all inter-related areas in development. Although research often examines the various areas separately, any one area of development affects all the other areas. This book is about sensory-motor development and so the focus is on that area. It must be understood, however, that movement within the environment influences cognitive and perceptual processing; perceptual processing is critical to movement; in addition, certainly there is a time in development that cognitive abilities become important to both of the other areas. There are many theories of human development but the most recent theory of dynamical systems explains that the emergence of developmental milestones is due to the interaction between the various developing systems and the external environment.[5] In this book, I am addressing the external environmental impacts on the developing child. This book deals in simplistic concepts so they can be communicated effectively and quickly to busy parents.

The most basic blocks of the foundation are prenatal experiences. These prenatal experiences will be discussed in the next chapter. For now it is important to note that prenatal experiences form the foundation for the development of skills known as motor milestones.[12] There are many developmental charts listing milestones for certain motor skills. The age the child reaches these milestones is not as important as the following sequential progression:

1. Baby tolerates being on tummy and begins lifting head off the surface.
2. Baby moves arms and legs while on tummy and can maintain contact of arms and legs with the surface.
3. Baby begins supporting upper body when lying on tummy and lifting head upright.
4. Baby begins rolling from tummy to back and back to tummy.
5. Baby begins to move on the floor while on tummy.
6. Baby pushes onto extended arms while on tummy.
7. Baby gets into a sitting position independently.
8. Baby gets onto hands and knees and begins to rock. (Often #7 and #8 occur at the same time or they reverse which comes first.)
9. Baby begins to creep on hands and knees.
10. Baby begins pulling to stand.
11. Baby begins to cruise walk sideways, holding onto furniture.
12. Baby begins taking independent steps.

With most babies, this progression is complete in about 15 months. Since a child has a lifetime to be upright, this interval of time in development is crucial for filling in the background foundation with skills that are not upright. These skills that are learned before the child is upright are critical foundational skills. When the baby is spending a lot of time on his tummy, he is building neck and back strength. During those times when the baby is lying on his tummy and moving his hand along the floor or crib mattress, important connections for eye hand coordination are being made. Belly crawling and creeping on hands and knees require coordination between the arm and leg on opposite sides of the body. This communication and coordination of the two sides of the brain are critical for many future skills concerning coordination as well as cognition. During the time baby is creeping on hands and knees there are sensory receptors being stimulated in the palm of the hand to reinforce where the hand is in space. At this same time the visual system is making a connection to understand how far away the hand is from the eye. This is information that is useful to the nervous system for all future eye-hand skills.

Children have the ability to skip steps and go ahead quickly. We may even see babies delight in sensory-motor experiences that are inappropriate for their stage of development. Just because a baby is having fun and being stimulated does not mean the activity is appropriate for their development. Sometimes, this results in a less sturdy foundation. Parents are being influenced to push their children ahead at faster rates of development. This push begins when children are infants. Toy and baby equipment marketers have had a strong influence in this push toward more advanced experiences for children, even in their infant and toddler stages. The Bumbo® chair is a good example of equipment placing a child in a sitting position supporting only the pelvis long before the child's development is ready to sit. Furthermore, we have almost an entire generation that is skipping the motor milestone of belly crawling due to the "Back to Sleep" campaign that was initiated in 1992 by the American Academy of Pediatrics. Since 1992, doctors have recommended that babies be placed on their backs to sleep to reduce the risk of Sudden Infant Death Syndrome (SIDS). Unfortunately, too many parents are interpreting this to mean that placing their baby on his tummy during the day is also not recommended. Since the "Back to Sleep" campaign was begun deaths by SIDS has been reduced by approximately 40%, [11] and along with that benefit has come at least two negative outcomes for millions of children. The first is that the incidence of plagiocephaly (misshapen skull) has increased from 1 in 300 before the "Back to Sleep" campaign to current estimates of 1 in 10![62] This negative outcome is influenced by babies being placed in "containers" (infant seats, swings, and other positioning devices) for extended periods of time during the day. This will be discussed more in later chapters. The second negative outcome is that research shows that babies are not being put on their tummies often enough during the day for them to develop the motor skills obtained from tummy time that were being obtained prior to the "Back to Sleep" campaign.[6,38,41,44]

At the same time that current child rearing practices are providing environments that encourage skipping developmental milestones, there exists a cultural explosion of increased visual and auditory stimulation for young children. Not enough people are asking if this cultural and technological explosion can be harmful to babies and young children. Some have questioned if cognitively pushing a baby very early is a waste of time, but parents do not usually worry about that. If there is even a slight possibility that it will be helpful, most parents are willing to invest the time and money to give it a try. It is important to examine the possibility that certain activities might actually be detrimental to a child's overall FUTURE development. It is equally important to ask what activities actually facilitate the development of strong and sturdy blocks in a child's foundation.

Understanding the concept of "sensory-motor" is crucial in learning to evaluate the impact of activities on a child's development. "Sensory" refers to what we perceive. It is the information coming into our bodies. "Motor" refers to how we respond to that input with our muscles. The blocks that are essential to the foundation for development and learning are built of sensory-motor information. The sensory-motor system far exceeds the most complex computer systems (an input-output system) imaginable.

The sensory, or perceptual, system can be aware of sensations coming in, such as visual images, sounds, tastes, smells, and touches. There are also many sensations, of which we are not consciously aware, that affect our system. Some examples are pressure on muscles and bones, joint position senses, amount of friction on the skin, stretch on tendons, body position in space, and related patterns of movement. In the womb, there are very basic sensory-motor experiences, such as being curled in the fetal position, being surrounded by total darkness, feeling wet and slick, and hearing the sound of the mother's heart beating. Other experiences are built upon these womb experiences, such as right after birth when the body stretches out for the first time, sees white light, feels dry skin sensations, and hears airborne noises.

These few examples are but a drop in a vast ocean of sensory-motor experiences. The foundation actually begins before the womb. At the moment of conception, a baby is given much sensory-motor information through the genetic code.[7] The most important point to understand is that there is an advantage to having a child experience as much of the sensory-motor progression as possible. This fills in the foundation blocks for learning. By filling in more of the early sensory-motor experiences, a child's foundation will be more solid.

How important are foundations? Instinctively we know they are very important . . . critical even. We know it by examples everywhere. The building industry is one example. Design engineering on the foundation as well as the exact materials to be used are much more critical than the design of the rooms or the faucets picked out for the bathroom. If not enough attention is paid to the design and materials for the foundation, the rest of the house will not matter. If the foundation cracks or the house falls down the fancy things done inside the house will be of little value.

Nature tells us that foundations are critically important also. We once had a Chinese Elm tree in our yard. We have flood irrigation, so the ground gets very wet, very deeply. Every time we would get any significant wind after irrigation, this tree would fall over. The next morning my husband would have to go out and prop it up. The tree kept getting bigger, with more branches and more leaves. It was growing into a beautiful tree, but it kept falling over in winds. The problem was the foundation of the tree. It didn't have a very good root structure. One day my husband got tired of propping the tree up, plus it was now a two man operation to get this big tree upright, so he chopped it to the ground. He didn't want to see that tree anymore. For a few years, some sprouts would pop out of the ground where the tree used to be, but my husband just went over it with the mower. Eventually, he decided to let the sprouts live and today, 15 years later, this tree is 40 feet tall and 40 feet wide. It is one of the most beautiful trees I have ever seen. No Arizona wind is taking this tree down now! The difference is that this tree focused its resources and nutrition on growing a healthy root structure for its foundation which allowed it to grow tall and strong.

This same foundation principle applies to child development. By understanding what skills are necessary for a sturdy foundation we can better prepare our children for the winds of life and better help them to achieve their potential for higher skills. No one has a perfect and complete foundation. This book is not written for the purpose of trying to achieve any sort of perfection or super child. By putting some attention on the foundation for a child and understanding key principles of development, parents can have a positive impact on the future of their child's abilities. By helping to build a more complete foundation, a child will be better able to handle stress and gain more skills. A solid sensory motor foundation is critical!

Chapter 2

Keys for Good Sensory-Motor Development

Before beginning to make the decisions necessary to build a good foundation in a child, it is necessary to have a plan. Good structures are always built using a blueprint. This blueprint helps to guide the process. In the same way, there are key principles of development that will help guide building a solid sensory-motor foundation. *Building Babies Better* has six keys that will lead to good choices for building a child's foundation. Understanding these keys will lead to less stress for the parent. The parent will understand the dynamics of the child's environment and activities and more easily make good choices.

Key #1
Reinforce previous sensory-motor experiences.

Repetition of previously learned sensory-motor experiences is beneficial to help a baby organize higher-level skills. It not only reinforces a learned skill but also develops endurance for that skill. Because the circuitry is already in place, repeating these activities often produces a calm and reorganized nervous system.

Adults unknowingly employ this principle when they need to "regroup". When they are trying to learn a more complex task, they find it helpful to go back to a task that is simple for them. For example, a tennis player having trouble with his game will return to basic strokes to regain coordination and confidence. Athletic coaches understand this principle well. They know that the basics are critical and time is never wasted going over them. Similarly, when infants are upset and crying, they often calm to the sound of a heartbeat, being cuddled in the fetal position, or even being patted in a heartbeat rhythm. Infants understand these sensations from being in the womb. This provides a point of reference that helps them to organize and calm.

Previous sensory-motor experiences from the womb include:

- Darkness
- Slickness
- Fetal position
- Heart beat sound
- Warmth (body temperature)
- Wet skin rubbing against own body and against the uterine wall
- Muscle sensations when pushing against resistance of the uterine wall
- Deep pressure sensations from being squeezed through the birth canal

Chapter one outlines the progression of motor experiences in the first year of life. The key to helping lay down this critical foundation is to provide opportunities for sensory-motor activities from stages the child has previously experienced. If a baby is struggling to get into sitting by himself or sits with a curved back instead of a straight back, the activities that are the most helpful are those previously learned activities. These would include spending more time on the floor belly crawling or improving muscle sensation using a massage technique that will be explained in the following chapters. This baby does not need more time in sitting to help with the skill of sitting.

If the baby understood all of the previously learned skills, sitting would come automatically.

Key #2

Gross motor comes before fine motor.

Big muscles (gross motor) need to learn how to work first so they can provide a good base of control for the little muscles (fine motor). In general, the big muscles are in the trunk (abdomen and back), shoulders, and hips. It is important for them to be strong and coordinated so that the hands and feet can work properly. The large muscles of the body also provide a stable base (postural control) from which the arms and legs can move. If the emphasis is placed on working on the coordination of hands and fingers before the trunk, shoulders, and hips are strong and coordinated, a baby's foundation may be compromised.

An example in a baby would be a child who is propped up in a high chair (before he can sit by himself) and placing an emphasis on picking up small bits of food on the tray. This child is being asked to coordinate a fine motor task before the gross motor foundation is complete and the body is stable in sitting.

An example in a preschool child would be asking a child to work on fine motor skills, such as cutting with scissors and paper/pencil tasks, when this child is having difficulty sitting in a chair or showing some difficulties in climbing or other gross motor skills. Often when a child has a short attention span for an activity or fatigues quickly, it is due to a poor foundation of skills leading up to the requested skill. A gross motor skill is a foundation skill to a fine motor task.

An important ability, especially for a preschool child, is focusing attention on the skill, such as cutting or paper/pencil tasks, and not on sitting still and controlling posture. If the foundation of gross motor (trunk muscles) is solid before the requirement of high level fine motor skills, the child's system experiences less stress because posture is automatic. If the foundation for posture is not solid, attention by the child is required for both posture and the skill, resulting too often in the attention to the task being lost or compromised.[17]

It is important to try to build a good gross motor foundation before fine motor skills are emphasized. Note that the term emphasized is used here because there is most likely no harm in exposing children to fine motor tasks before the gross motor foundation is solid as long as it is understood that the activity should be brief and no expectations are made on the precision of the fine motor activity. The goal is to have the skills performed well and with the least amount of system stress. For that, the gross motor foundation must be solid. When making a choice between a gross motor activity and a fine motor activity for a baby or young child, the best choice is the gross motor activity. Placing an emphasis on gross motor is a key to success!

Key #3

Allow baby to grow into higher skills.

If a child is having difficulty with a particular skill, the source of the problem is not with that skill. Instead, the foundation up to that point is not complete. If the foundation is complete, learning is instantaneous. Building the foundation is a gradual process.

Perhaps a child is having difficulty with a skill: either his frustration level is too high or he is not able to do the skill. In responding to this difficulty, the previous skills must be considered. The best approach is to step back to a related, previous sensory-motor skill that the child was able to achieve. After repeating that skill for a while, the child may be able to perform the higher skill more easily. Often the child will go back to a previous skill at various times in development. When learning to creep on hands and knees, babies are often seen moving across the floor in two different modes of travel, both belly crawling and creeping. Babies tend to revert back to their own previously learned motor skills when the need arises. This is natural. Once the background is understood, belly crawling will be replaced completely by the creeping on hands and knees.

In these first years of life, especially through the preschool and kindergarten years, learning should go smoothly and with as little stress as possible. The learning should be child-driven. An example of this principle is a baby whose parents think he is ready to sit on his own. When placed in a sitting position, the baby shows a rounded back and easily loses balance in any direction. This baby is not ready for sitting. To build the background, this baby needs to be down crawling on his belly because this builds background sensory motor skills necessary for good sitting. The baby also needs to learn to move up and down off low surfaces to challenge his balance while he is on his tummy. This foundation is necessary for the strength and balance of sitting. In this example, it is not helpful to continually practice sitting to achieve better sitting. It is appropriate, however, to provide more opportunities for the baby to crawl and be on his tummy. There is a "readiness" aspect to a baby's developing system. Babies are not mini-adults. Often, parents make decisions based on what they would like or what they feel would be entertaining or fun. A baby reacts to his environment differently than an adult would react to that same environment. It is clear in the study of development that each system has a rate at which it develops.[20] Not all systems in a baby are in the "ready" state. When this readiness of the system is factored into development, it becomes clear that development should progress in a self-organizing manner. The activities in this book take into account the readiness of a baby's system for each particular activity. Allow baby to grow into higher skills, DON'T PUSH!

Key #4

Encourage activities that use both sides of the body.

Encouraging the use of activities that utilize both hands before specializing in activities that require the use of one hand is beneficial for building a good sensory-motor foundation. Using the body bilaterally (both sides together) is more basic than using the body unilaterally (one side more specialized).[23,24] An example of using this key with a baby is providing larger toys that require the use of both hands rather than primarily small toys that are easily picked up with one hand. Observe how the baby plays with his toys. If a baby likes to hold a stuffed animal by the tag and finger play with the tag instead of holding the animal with both hands and cuddling it, cut off the tag to encourage bilateral play. For a preschool child, an example is not introducing scissor skills until he has mastered tearing paper with two hands proficiently. Small toys not only use primarily one hand instead of involving both sides, but small toys also require more of a fine motor emphasis rather than a gross motor emphasis. (Key #2 Gross motor comes before fine motor.)

Key #5

Avoid small, detailed visual images.

Vision is the most "primitive" sensory system at birth when compared to all the other sensory systems.[30] The visual processing areas of our brain are not even close to maturity until after seven months of age and maturity isn't complete until around age eight. The development of fine, detailed vision begins gradually around six months of age and is complete around five years of age. It appears that all the other sensory systems mature before vision, so vision works off a foundation of all the other sensations. For this discussion, there are two different aspects of vision. The earliest visual abilities to develop have to do with peripheral vision (off to the sides), detecting motion and orientation in space. This is important to orient to mother's face, detect when something is coming at the baby and, with the vestibular system, to help in head control and stabilizing gaze. However, looking at specific visual images such as toys is the aspect of vision that requires the focal area of the eye and matures gradually over the first eight years of life.

The one area of the brain that is relatively more mature at birth is the sensory-motor processing area. This is due to the positions, movements, and skin contact stimulation the fetus experienced in the womb environment. The nervous system has a chronological order to the maturation of the sensory system. The areas of the sensory system that are the most mature have the most impact on the movement system. Prior to age six months the most mature sensory system is the system that includes touch and skin sensations. It is not until around the age of six months, when baby is crawling and goal directed towards a toy or person, that vision begins to function in a more mature way thereby having more of an impact on movement. In the author's experience as a pediatric therapist, if a baby is too visually stimulated early in life, the foundation for other sensations, such as skin sensations, may be compromised. An example of this is a baby that has a mobile and other toys in the crib, toys hanging over the infant carrier, and toys over a toy bar. With an emphasis on strong visual stimulation, the baby may not tune in to other sensations such as skin or muscle. Young babies who spend much time in equipment that hold them upright, such as infant seats and jumpers, have been observed demonstrating much visual attention to activity around them. Often when these same babies are put on the floor in the prone position, they do not move their arms and legs against the surface and often do not tolerate the position because it reduces their visual input and they are not content with the sensory environment of skin on floor or muscles moving. Even after the age of six months, vision can interfere with the processing of more basic sensory motor skills

Vision is a very important and very controlling sensation. There is a time for emphasis in this area, but early in a child's life is not the proper time. A baby has plenty of opportunity for visual stimulation. The baby's favorite and most recognized visual image is his parent's face. Hopefully baby gets a lot of that stimulation. Baby's brain is organized in such a way that certain shapes are recognized in his brain at certain stages of development. This recognition is easy for baby and does not push visual stimulation too early or too much. There will be more discussion in the following chapters on the visual system as it relates to a solid sensory motor foundation.

Vision at a distance is a more relaxed function than close, detailed vision. This is true at all ages in development. The early years should be spent moving on the floor and, when old enough, playing outdoors, which provides opportunities to use vision at a far point, plus gives the added benefit of coordinating movement with our vision. Today's children spend much time looking at detailed images on a computer screen or television. Even when they have the opportunity to use their vision at a distance when they are riding in the car, they now have DVD's to watch, so that opportunity is lost!

A study done with one-year-old and three-year-old children found a correlation between time spent in front of a television and negative effects on brain development.[25] The authors of this study speculated that watching television makes changes in the wiring of the developing brain, which is undergoing rapid growth in the first few years of life. The authors suggested a correlation between the amount of television exposure and the risk of attention deficit hyperactivity disorder, ADHD. The lead author felt that because of the young age of the children, it was not the television content, but the fast paced visual images that altered brain development.

One should be cautious when stimulating a baby visually, and must understand that turning on and over-stimulating the visual system at a young age contributes to a less sturdy foundation for future development. When faced with a choice of an activity where the child is primarily looking at small, detailed images or actively involved in moving his body and looking at larger images, the best choice is to avoid small, detailed visual images!

Key #6
Play within limits of fatigue.

This key is the most difficult key principle to understand, but once understood will considerably help parenting skills even into the teenage years! Often fatigue is understood as being tired and needing sleep. This is certainly one concept of fatigue. The concept of fatigue in this key principle, however, is something much more. For every activity a baby engages in, he has a certain number of circuits in his nervous system for performing that activity with efficiency and coordination. For the sake of simplicity, consider for this example that a baby has three different circuits at the age of two weeks that allows that baby to lift his head up when being held on the parent's shoulder. These circuits are short in duration at this level of development and only last briefly. Baby holds his head up for a few seconds, tires and repeats this two more times. But on the fourth try baby wobbles, arches and struggles more to lift the head. The head still comes up, but it looks less coordinated. At this point the system has fatigued and until the original three circuits recover, the coordination is lost and effort needed for the activity increases. The key principle here is to play (perform the activity) within the time that the activity has the most coordination and least effort and to stop the activity when the coordination level goes down.

Here is another example. Parent and baby are playing on the floor. Baby gets into the sitting position and the parent starts to engage baby in play with a toy while baby is sitting. For the first minute or two the baby's back looks straight and baby's sitting balance is sufficient for him to reach out and touch the toy. After the first minute, baby's back becomes more rounded and more effort is needed to reach out and touch the toy. When the back begins to round, fatigue is present.

In a preschool age child an example would be when the child is playing catch with a large ball. For the first two attempts the child catches and throws with ease, but soon the child is arching his back to throw and begins throwing in the wrong direction. Again, fatigue has set in after two attempts.

The principle behind Key #6, Play within limits of fatigue, is for the adult to recognize when the activity has fatigued and change the activity briefly while the system recovers. It is much better to have effortless and coordinated movement reinforced rather than reinforcing less coordinated movement. Often parents do this automatically. In the example of holding the baby on the parent's shoulder and the system fatigue produces a wobbly baby, parents naturally shift position or hold the baby in front of them for awhile. In the example of the baby sitting and then the posture begins to sag, it would be best to lay the baby on his tummy to play for a short while and then the child can resume playing in sitting. In the example of the preschool child playing ball, it would be beneficial for the child to take a short break when the signs of fatigue begin. The short break does not need to be a rest; it could be a change of activity. The child could catch the ball until signs of fatigue set in and the adult could roll the ball a few times or ask the child to see how high he can jump. Any activity that is different from the one that showed signs of fatigue would be helpful.

Many reading this book at this point may feel this principle goes too far. How can a parent constantly be watching children for signs of fatigue and monitor their activities so closely? This is not expected and it is not helpful to even attempt that. It is very beneficial to children if their parents understand this principle. Many parents feel that the more the better is the key principle with all activities for children. They mistakenly believe that practice makes perfect in all situations. By understanding that building the background is what makes movement and coordination better and not practicing at a high level of function, stress will be reduced for both the parent and the child.

Recognize signs of fatigue (change in posture, increased effort expenditure, rubbing the eyes, and lack of interest to name a few). When signs of fatigue are present, changing the activity will be helpful. One must remember that short, appropriate activities are beneficial for building a solid sensory motor foundation in a baby and young child. The other 5 key principles point to which activities are appropriate. This key principle gives a guideline for how long to stay at an activity.

Understanding these six key principles provides a basis for evaluating whether an activity has a positive or negative effect on sensory-motor development at a certain time in a child's life. The following chapters contain more information about each of these keys and how to apply them at various stages of development.

The Six Keys for Good Sensory-Motor Development

Key#1 Reinforce previous sensory-motor experiences.

Key #2 Gross motor comes before fine motor.

Key #3 Allow baby to grow into higher skills.

Key #4 Encourage activities that use both sides of the body.

Key #5 Avoid small, detailed visual images.

Key #6 Play within limits of fatigue.

Part I

Early Infancy
Birth through Six Months

What an exciting time! The miracle of birth is beyond description! Once the awe starts to dissipate, the awareness of the baby's need for nourishment and sleep becomes paramount. Typically, little attention is paid to the baby's sensory-motor needs at this time. Most decisions are made on the basis of what will make the baby most comfortable. During this time, as a baby is adjusting to a tremendous change in environment, one can easily begin to build a solid foundation by reinforcing previous sensory-motor experiences. This will provide the baby with the opportunity to fill in missing information in some basic foundation blocks. If the information is already in the baby's foundation, by reinforcing previous sensory-motor experiences, the baby will calm because this is familiar territory for him.

Reinforce previous sensory-motor experiences.
What are some of these previous sensory-motor experiences? In the womb, the baby was in an extremely dark, wet, warm environment. The baby was in the fetal flexion position (curled and tucked) and could never fully stretch out his body. The primary sound that the baby heard, the mother's heartbeat, was rhythmical in nature. There are many more prenatal sensory-motor experiences in the baby's background that are critical to his development, but the focus here is on the baby being in darkness, wetness, warmth, and in a curled position.

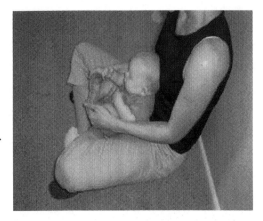

This three-month-old boy is in the fetal flexion position. In the womb this position would be much tighter, but he is demonstrating how all of his joints are in flexion.

After birth, it is essential for the baby to learn to succeed in his new environment, which is radically different from the prenatal environment. To name a few differences, the baby now has to move against gravity, adjust his own body temperature, hear airborne noises, suck for nourishment, and fully extend his body. The world is full of stimulation at this point. The baby has a whole world to see, and new sounds are constantly bombarding him. These first six months are a time when the more basic sensory-motor systems are trying to organize to provide the proper foundation for higher skills, such as sitting, babbling, eating solid foods, and crawling. Organizing the more basic functions, not pushing forward toward higher skills, is critical at this time. The more basic functions include an understanding of sensations, such as pressure into bones and muscle, light touch on the skin, overall body positioning, individual movement patterns of the arms and legs, and a correlation of the hands with the eyes.

Allow baby to grow into higher skills.

The activities and recommendations outlined in the following chapters will enhance the foundation of sensory-motor experiences. The most important factor during this time is not how to make the baby's environment more stimulating, but how to assist the baby to be calmed and handle the stimulation that is already present. During this developmental stage a little work goes a long way. In other words, trying to fill in information in the blocks is much easier and successful at this stage than at any other.

Chapter 3

Feeding Considerations

The subject of feeding is a broad one. This book will not attempt to address all of the feeding issues, but will instead focus on the positioning that will build a strong sensory-motor foundation.

This mother is using a good technique for feeding her daughter a bottle. The baby has both of her arms in front so she can hold her bottle if she wishes. Mom is making eye contact and alternates sides for each feeding.

Encourage activities that use both sides of the body.

Be sure to feed a baby by holding him in a semi-reclined position on different sides at different feedings. This occurs naturally if a child is being breast fed. However, many bottle-fed babies get used to one side only. Experiencing each side is important to their sensory-motor system for several reasons. For one, a different arm is positioned outward and has more freedom of movement. Both of baby's arms should be forward so that one arm is not trapped behind the mother. This allows for baby's posture to be more symmetrical and also gives the baby the opportunity to use both hands together. Having both hands together in the midline of his body is necessary so that he can eventually hold his own bottle or cup. Hands in midline help establish good communication between the two sides of the brain.

The position of a baby's neck is another reason to change sides at different feedings. A baby will tend to look outward while feeding and needs the opportunity to do so on both sides. Changing feeding sides also affects a baby's oral motor experience. The nipple sits differently in the mouth depending on which side the baby is held. The muscles in the mouth respond differently depending on where the nipple sits in the mouth. The muscles used in the feeding process are the same muscles used for speech. When attention is paid to changing sides during feeding, the muscles have a better opportunity for full development. By changing sides during bottle-feeding, an opportunity for "balanced" sensory input on both sides of the body is created.

Not only does a baby look outward during feeding time, but this is also a special time for baby to have eye-to-eye contact with their parent. The best visual input for a baby is staring into the eyes of his parent. Chapter 23 will discuss further benefits of this eye-to-eye contact in the parent-child bonding process.

Chapter 4

Visual Environment during Early Infancy

During these next two chapters the importance of the baby's visual and auditory environment throughout early infancy will be examined. A visit to a toy or baby store or most babies' homes will demonstrate that the "more is better" philosophy is definitely in practice when it comes to visual and auditory stimulation. This author's experience has taught that the opposite is true. The philosophy that should prevail during the first few months of a baby's life is—avoid visual and auditory clutter. The most important visual stimulation a baby needs is his parent's face. The most important auditory stimulation a baby needs is his parent's voice. The value of spending time face to face with a baby can never be underestimated!

The concept of providing more stimulation for a baby must be examined carefully. Reading the baby's cues, especially during the first few months, is crucial. One of the best skills to be developed by a parent is to understand when a baby is over-stimulated. Very young babies often demonstrate this by crying, turning away, shutting down, or falling asleep. Parents often mistakenly assume that their baby is tolerating a very noisy, stimulating environment because he sleeps all the time. Instead, this baby is trying to tell them that he cannot handle the stimulation and needs to check out. Although avoiding over-stimulation at all times is impossible, the goal is to monitor how much of the baby's day is spent in this type of environment and to keep it to a minimum. Good development is difficult to achieve in an overly stimulated environment. Frequently the child's system becomes disorganized during highly stimulating times.

Over the years, the babies who have spent time in the Neonatal Intensive Care Unit (NICU) have taught the importance of their sleep environment. In years past the NICU was very noisy and had bright white lights on 24 hours a day. This was necessary due to the required monitoring and procedures being performed. In time, the hospital staff has learned that a dark and quiet environment is beneficial for babies, and they have made great improvements in improving the NICU environment in recent years.

> I worked with one baby, Seth, who came home from the hospital, having spent months in the NICU, and could only fall asleep if the lights and radio were on in his room. Seth tended to be a bit irritable, and his movements lacked good flexion (movements toward being curled in a fetal position). He arched his back and extended his legs frequently. Seth's mother and I established a program of weaning him from the lights and radio in his room. It took many months for this baby boy to be able to sleep in a dark, quiet room. When this was accomplished, Seth's irritability decreased, and he curled in the fetal position more often. (Deep sleep and fetal flexion posture are learned in the womb in total darkness. Key #2 Reinforce previous sensory-motor experiences.) By focusing on his visual and auditory environment, as well as other basic blocks of his sensory-motor foundation, both his mother and I felt the changes we made contributed to his later resiliency and good disposition.

The Crib

The crib is a place where a baby calms, sleeps, and moves. The goal is to create a soothing and relaxing crib environment. Sleep researchers working with adults recommend that the bedroom be a place for sleep only, with no television and especially no paperwork from the office. In this way, the nervous system associates the bed with relaxation and sleep; sleep, thus, comes more easily. Applying these same principles to the crib, there should be no mirrors, mobiles, or other toys. Try to create a place of relaxation, not stimulation. When baby wakes he will tune in more to sensations of his skin and muscles if the crib environment is not visually stimulating. Because babies are now sleeping on their backs and they tend to turn towards the door, it is best to alternate the end of the crib on which the baby's head is placed to avoid excessive pressure on one side of the skull.

Avoid small, detailed visual images.

Start with pastel colors, and avoid using printed crib sheets and bumper pads. The designs on most sheets and bumper pads are small and detailed. The visual environment of the crib should not be stimulating. If the parent enjoys the printed, busy patterns, place them where the adults can enjoy them and keep them away from the baby's visual field. Turn the bumper pads so that the plain side is toward the baby and the printed side is on the outside. Paint the upper part of the walls a plain, soft color, and use the busy wallpaper for lower areas that the baby cannot see while lying in the crib. Do not place any visually stimulating items in the crib; especially do not place mirrors and mobiles in the crib.

A baby who is visually entertained all of the time may seem more visually attentive, but this is not the goal for this stage. During this time, the goal is to help organize and enhance the baby's more basic systems, such as touch, pressure, and movement. If a baby is content just looking around, the chances of tuning in to the other sensations are diminished. A baby learns so much by moving his arms and legs on the bed surface. Important eye-hand functions are improved when a baby spends time looking at his own hand. Rolling and the beginning of belly crawling are usually skills perfected while the baby is in his crib. All of these activities take place more frequently when a baby is not overly visually stimulated. The goal is not to entertain, but to provide an environment where the baby can learn the most about his body.

Dark Room

Another visual consideration in the baby's room is the use of a night-light. When a night-light is used all night, a different type of rest will occur than when the baby sleeps without any light on and is in total darkness. Even when the baby's eyes are closed, the nervous system can pick up the difference between light and dark. The most beneficial sleep comes in an environment of total darkness, exactly like when the baby first slept in his mother's womb.

> I once worked with a two-year-old boy, Josh, who had never slept through the night. Josh had some developmental problems and was born prematurely. Going to sleep had become a nightmare for him and his mother. She was exhausted and tried her best to calm him when he awoke at night, but he would only sleep for about two hours before she had to get up with him again. I began to utilize the keys to building a solid sensory-motor foundation. In particular, it appeared that Josh did not understand fetal flexion (the curled up position) because he cried whenever we tried to hold him in this position. Generally when a baby does not tolerate a position well it is because the sensory-motor foundation for that position is not complete. We focused on doing deep pressure, (a massage technique that will be explained later), having no night-light, and holding him in the dark in the fetal position with the heartbeat sound on. In two months, this fitful child was sleeping through the night!

If a night-light is needed for the parent's use to get up with the baby in the night, then use a night-light on a switch with a 25-watt blue light bulb. The parent can then switch on the night-light while attending to the baby and switch it off when finished. Instead of a white light bulb in a lamp or overhead light, using a 25-watt blue light bulb gives sufficient light to attend to baby's needs and also continues to provide a relaxing environment that allows baby to get back to sleep. A blue 25-watt light bulb can be found at most grocery stores or home improvement centers.

Rest in total darkness is essential for a baby. If he is already trained to sleep with a light on all the time or if he is irritated by total darkness, a program of "weaning" him from a night-light is valuable. This is accomplished by using a 25-watt blue light bulb while the baby falls asleep. When he falls asleep, the light is then turned off. Once a baby is falling asleep in blue light, then it is time to begin having him fall asleep in darkness. Falling asleep in total darkness is preferable at night. Research shows that taking naps in the day in dim, indirect light is not as disruptive to good sleep as using light during night time sleep.[35]

It is essential that the baby's room be totally dark. If a streetlight is glaring into the window, black out shades or some other window covering may be needed. It is helpful to do a darkness check in the baby's room. This can be done by sitting in the room in the darkness. In less than one minute the eyes adjust to less light; the darkness of the room can then be assessed. It is amazing how often rooms that initially appear dark actually have sources of light through the windows or under the doors.

Most babies begin to enjoy total darkness. Many babies and young children are content in their cribs for relatively long periods of time after they have awakened in total darkness. During this time, they are not visually "turned on" and spend much valuable time exploring and developing other sensations, such as touch, hearing, and movement.

Why are other sensations more easily perceived when vision is not being used? Picture yourself at a crowded party. The environment is so busy and noisy that you do not even notice when someone brushes up against you. Now imagine that you are in a dark, quiet room. Someone brushes up against you again. Which situation would make you relate to the sensation of touch more? The clear answer is the one in which you were in the dark, quiet room. It is important to balance your child's developmental background and provide opportunities when he is visually stimulated, as well as times when he is not. A typical day provides much visual stimulation and so the effort needs to be placed on times where there is less visual stimulation.

Sleeping in total darkness is vital to a good rest that will be beneficial to the nervous system. Spending time in the dark actually enhances visual function by allowing the visual system to better understand contrast. Contrast is the difference between dark and light, which is essential to good visual function. Having a baby spend time awake in a quiet, dark or dimly lit environment not only enhances the development of the visual system but other sensory systems as well.

Chapter 5

Auditory Environment during Early Infancy

Heartbeat

 ***Reinforce previous sensory-motor experiences.***
One must consider the sounds in a baby's environment. It is crucial to remember that one of the goals is to reinforce previous sensory-motor experiences. One of a baby's previous experiences is listening to his mother's heartbeat.

Hearing the heartbeat sound during the first six months of life is a beneficial activity for all babies.

There are many devices that produce a heartbeat sound, but not all heartbeat recordings are alike. It is important to get a heartbeat recording that simulates a real adult heartbeat sound and does not add music to it. One mother found a website by searching "heartbeat sound" and was able to download a wonderful recording. A local baby store will probably have a stuffed bear or positioning wedge with a white box in it (by Dex®) that holds a heartbeat recording that has proven helpful with many babies. Some babies become irritable with certain recordings and quiet with others. For other babies, the heartbeat sound always makes them irritable. There are many reasons for this. One reason may be "empty" blocks in their foundation. Therefore, the sound is not well understood by the nervous system. Another possible reason is that the rhythmical sound is a strong sensation, and their systems may already be on overload when they hear it.

If a baby becomes irritated by the heartbeat sound more than three times, try another recording. If that does not help, try holding the baby in a dimly lit room while listening to the heartbeat. Short exposures are helpful. Do not force this sound on a baby if the irritability continues. In addition to this sound reinforcing a previous sensory-motor experience, the rhythmical nature of the heartbeat may be the foundation for future skills requiring rhythm and sequence, such as music and math.

This mother is demonstrating holding her baby in tight flexion. This position is similar to one the baby was in while in the womb. The white box is the heartbeat sound device that is found inside some teddy bears that are available commercially. Holding a baby in tight flexion in a dimly lit or dark room, while listening to the heartbeat, reinforces previous sensory-motor experiences. This activity often calms a baby and will facilitate better sleep.

Music

What other considerations should be given to the auditory environment of a baby's room? Music is great for playtime. Some think that playing classical music has an impact on intelligence. The only caution concerning this is that classical music is complex. This complexity is not lost on the baby's nervous system. Because building a solid foundation before going up the pyramid of complexity is so essential, providing classical music for a very young child, especially an infant, is not appropriate. As grandmothers of the past have known, music that is simple in nature, such as lullabies and repetitive children's songs, is more appropriate.

Quiet

The most valuable consideration for the auditory environment of a baby's room is to be sure there are periods of quiet. When any noise is present, the nervous system will pay attention to it. Quiet times are needed for good rest. It is a good idea to check the room for noise by just sitting in the dark in the room. Is a clock or a high-pitched whine of an air conditioner heard? High-pitched noises seem to be the most disruptive. This is probably due to the fact that in the womb hearing begins in the low frequency ranges. One should try to eliminate as many noises as possible.

Chapter 6

Tummy Time Activity

During the first few months of life, it is essential for babies to spend awake time lying on their tummies. In 1992, doctors began recommending babies not sleep on their tummies due to the risk of Sudden Infant Death Syndrome (SIDS). They have called this program "Back to Sleep" and, since its inception, the death rate of infants due to SIDS has dropped by about 40 %.[11]However, because of this program, many parents are now afraid to put their babies on their tummies at all. This has had a negative impact on the development of infants.

By not putting babies on their tummies, some babies' heads will become flattened in the back or on the sides if the baby is in a hard plastic container, such as an infant seat, for extended periods of time. It is not clear whether this flattening is harmful to brain function, but most parents wish to avoid this problem. As described earlier, the incidence of flattening of the skull, or plagiocephaly, has increased significantly since the early 90's. Some estimates find the incidence as high as 1 or 2 in every 10 babies! [62] In addition to this potential problem, babies who are not put on their tummies lose opportunities to build neck and back muscle strength and coordination. The very best position in which to develop neck and back muscles is on the tummy. When baby lifts his head or even turns his head from side to side, the back muscles stabilize the body, and the muscles on both sides of the back learn to work together. This work, done by a baby during "tummy time", forms the foundation for sitting, standing and walking. It is one of the most valuable experiences a baby can have.

The solution for protecting a baby from SIDS and avoiding the negatives associated with keeping a baby on his back at all times is to provide supervised "tummy time". This is a time when a baby is placed on his tummy while an adult is watching him. It is recommended that you supervise tummy time at least during the first six months of a baby's life. Babies should be placed on their tummies while being supervised as young as right after birth.

> The parents of a beautiful baby girl, Laura, brought her to me when she was six weeks old. At the initial visit, her mother reported that Laura did not ever tolerate lying on her tummy. In fact, there were not many positions in which she was comfortable, and she was frequently irritable. The parents had tried to put her on her tummy on a blanket on the floor or couch. I recommended that they use a heavy piece of vinyl or plastic on top of their carpet. I also suggested that they use some grape-seed oil on the plastic under her arms and legs so she could move more easily on the plastic. Since the frequency of putting her on her tummy was more important than the length of time she spent there, we decided to put Laura on her tummy for a couple of minutes, two to three times each day. One week later, we got together to take pictures. The change was remarkable! Laura now loved being on her tummy and even posed quite nicely for a picture in that position. Her mother delightedly reported that Laura was now happier and more content. I suggested the family continue to increase tummy time each week until Laura was on her tummy for a total of one to one and a half hours per day.

This tummy time activity should be done on the floor in case a baby rolls. (Normally, rolling can start as early as two to three months of age.) Most of the time, babies are placed on their tummies on a blanket. It is best that a baby be on a smooth surface, such as a very heavy ply plastic, a piece of vinyl flooring or a mat. Moving arms and legs on a smooth surface instead of one that has more friction, such as carpet or a blanket, is a very different sensory-motor experience. To understand this difference, try lying on your tummy on the carpet and pulling your leg up to your side in a crawl movement. Keep in mind the effort and coordination required to do this. Now, do this same activity on a smooth surface, such as the plastic, vinyl, or mat described earlier. The smooth surface will require less effort, feel more coordinated, and give you a sense of wanting to repeat the activity again.

To create a smooth surface on which a baby can learn coordinated movement, a clean area of vinyl or wood floor can be used. (Tile does not work well for this activity.) It is best, however, to obtain a piece of heavy ply plastic (16 to 20 ply) or a piece of vinyl flooring. The heavy ply plastic can usually be found at fabric stores and comes in a roll that is clear. It can be purchased by the yard and one yard is enough for a small baby. The exact ply is not important. As long as it is thick enough to not bunch up when baby moves on it, it will work. The vinyl flooring is sold in 6-foot widths at flooring and home improvement stores. The best choice for flooring is one that is the smoothest and has the least design. The plastic comes in 45-inch widths. The minimum size for either type of flooring should be a 1-yard (3-foot) length. The plastic, therefore, would be 45 inches by 36 inches, and the vinyl flooring would be 36 inches by 6 feet. It may be wise to plan ahead for the time when the baby will be moving and crawling on his tummy by purchasing enough vinyl to cover an area in the family room or wherever the most time is spent in the home. The plastic or vinyl can then be put over the carpet and used as an "area rug" for the few months that a baby needs a smooth surface. Babies prefer the smooth surface to be a bit soft. If you are putting the plastic on a tile floor, put a blanket under the plastic. Baby can use this smooth surface for moving until the baby is creeping on hands and knees, which usually occurs around seven to nine months of age. When a baby is very young, the small piece of heavy ply plastic works well because it is easy to roll up and take along to see Grandma, drop baby off at the sitter's house, or even spend the afternoon in the park.

This five-month-old girl is playing on a surface of heavy ply plastic. Note she is wearing long sleeves and long pants so she can move more easily. Also note that she only has one toy to play with and it is placed slightly away from her so she must move to get it.

Now that the slick surface is in place, the fun begins! Remember that until a baby is six months of age this should be a supervised activity. If baby falls asleep on his tummy, he can be rolled onto his side or back so that he can continue to sleep.

By increasing the "slickness," the muscle coordination and sensory organization for crawling in enhanced. This can be done in one of two ways. First, baby could wear long-sleeved and long-legged clothes, such as pajamas with no feet in them. This makes it easier for his arms and legs to glide along the surface. Leaving the feet bare allows for some traction to propel forward in belly crawling.

An even better way to make the surface slick is to remove baby's clothes and apply some oil to the surface under his arms, legs, and belly. Any oil to which your baby is not allergic can be used, but here is a note of CAUTION: Some babies will have an allergic reaction to certain oils. Peanut oil is a highly allergic substance for some people so one should avoid it. Grape-seed oil works well with most babies. Using oils that are edible is preferred because baby will enjoy licking the surface during this activity. Before beginning this activity, test the oil that is planned to be used on a small area of the baby's skin. If there is any negative reaction, another lubricant will be needed. Also, be careful about the aroma of the oil. Using a lubricant with no additional fragrance is optimal. Clean up is necessary right after using oil to maintain a smooth surface. Using paper towels or disinfectant wipes works well.

Once a baby is on his tummy on this slick surface, it is wonderful to watch as he begins to lift his head off the surface and coordinates movements of his head from side to side, his arms up and down along the surface, and his legs in crawl movements. This is a time when a baby may even move forward or in a circle. Baby's developmental concepts will be enhanced as he is able to be content and explore in this position. A critical building block of enhancing skin sensations is accomplished during this activity. This exercise also builds his foundation and improves his muscle coordination.

A routine before placing a baby on his tummy can help towards the baby tolerating being in this position. The routine will become familiar and he can anticipate what is coming. Also it can be a bit of a sensory overload for some babies to all of sudden be placed on their tummies. Starting by placing a baby on his back on the prepared surface will help to begin the routine in a familiar position. This activity is all about the sensory experience, so it is important to prepare baby's tummy to feel the surface when he is turned on his tummy. The routine should start by gently rubbing the skin on his tummy and even helping him to rub his own tummy by taking his hand and rubbing it all over the tummy area. After a short time of this sensory experience (about 20 seconds), baby can be slowly rolled over and his parent can lie next to him. This should be a calm and positive sensory experience and toys should not be used at this time. If he is agitated, sometimes it is helpful for the parent to get close to him and gently reassure him with a soft voice. Each time this activity is done, the baby will tolerate it better. If necessary this activity can be short, perhaps one minute to start.

Tummy time should be done frequently throughout the day. By the age of four months, a baby should be spending a total time of at least one to two hours on his tummy each day. Each child's tolerance for tummy time is different. Once a baby enjoys being on his tummy, the baby will expand his time on his own. In an older baby, about 6 months of age, entering a toy into the environment can be enjoyable for the baby. Prior to that age the baby is content with feeling all the sensory experiences of moving arms and legs on the surface and lifting up his head. Caution should be used to not overly stimulate the baby with loud, flashy toys. One or two toys should be the most to enter into the baby's visual field.

Moving baby's arms and legs in a crawling pattern can be beneficial to help baby feel these movements and sensations. Crawl movements of the arms are done with the hand open on the surface and at shoulder level. The hand is moved up above the level of the head and back down near shoulder level. Crawl movements of the legs are done with the inside part of the leg in contact with the surface. The knee is moved up along side the trunk of the body and then moved back into a straight leg position. While moving the leg upward, the ankle is moved upward also. Do these exercises one arm or leg at a time, keeping as much of the inner surface of the limb on the floor as possible. It is good to repeat this on each arm and leg about ten times. If the baby's legs or arms are not contacting the surface, but are instead doing "airplane" movements in the air, occasionally and gently move his arms and legs in contact with the surface.

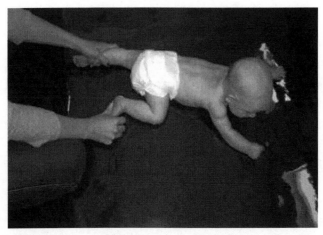

This mother and son are demonstrating the crawl movements of the leg. The baby is on a slick surface of oil on a heavy ply plastic mat. The mother is moving the leg upward while keeping the baby's leg in contact with the surface. It is best if the ankle is moved upward at the same time the knee is moved upward. The leg then returns to the starting extended position. This can also be done on a slick surface with clothes covering the baby's legs and arms rather than using oil.

This is not a time to stimulate a baby with toys. From birth to six months of age, babies need to play with their movements and touch sensations. They are trying to organize their very stimulating environment. Toys are more appropriate after six months of age. Let the baby learn to be content for a few minutes, learning to move his body. Don't give in to the temptation to try to get him to look at and move a toy at this stage. Instead, lay down on the floor with him and let him look at your face, his favorite visual stimulation! If a toy is used for stimulation, use only one toy and place it just out of reach so baby will begin to move towards it. Generally it is not until five to seven months that baby begins to move toward a toy.

Occasionally a baby is placed on his tummy over a pillow or rolled towel. By lifting the baby's upper trunk with the pillow or towel, the baby's action of lifting the head is easier and it encourages greater use of vision. Positioning on tummy with a rolled towel or pillow is not recommended because valuable sensory experiences are being omitted from the activity, and visual stimulation is not a focus at this stage of development. It is best for baby to be on his tummy directly on the smooth surface on the floor.

Tummy time is not difficult to incorporate into the day. Clean-ups from spitting up or leaky diapers are easy on the smooth surface. The necessary equipment is easy to transport. Simply roll it up and take it along!

Creativity goes a long way with babies. Remembering the principle that tummy time is so important, there are many ways to incorporate tummy time into baby's day. Having mom or dad lie on the floor with baby on his or her chest is always fun. Going on a walk while pulling baby in a wagon or pushing him in a pram while baby is on his tummy is another great way for one to include tummy time into the day.

Chapter 7

Tummy-Leg Rub Activity

 Reinforce previous sensory-motor experiences.
The tummy-leg rub is beneficial because it provides sensory input that is familiar to the baby from his experiences in the womb and helps to organize his nervous system. It will also facilitate the baby to release a tightly fisted hand, begin to understand sensations on the palm of his hand, and release any tight hip muscles. Lotion or oil can be used. (If you have not already done so, please make sure to read the CAUTION in Chapter 6.) Since this is a sensory experience that baby had in the womb, it can be started soon after birth. The main focus of this activity is for baby to relate to skin sensations. If you make eye contact with baby or do this in a highly visually stimulating environment, such as under a mobile, the baby's nervous system may pay more attention to the visual input than the skin input. During the actual rubbing of the arms and legs it is best to not have eye contact or entertain the baby. This activity only lasts one minute and afterwards smiles, praise, and songs would be great!

Tummy Rub

The tummy rub is best done with the infant's diaper off, while he is lying on his back. Spread some lubricant on the baby's tummy. Then, gently rub one of the baby's hands over his tummy. Be sure the baby's hand is in contact with the tummy and your hand is not interfering with that sensation. Do this slowly in all directions (side to side, up and down, and in circles). The baby's hand should open automatically so that the palm of the hand is touching the tummy. If the hand is closed, use your other hand to gently open his hand so that the palm can be in contact with his tummy. If you feel resistance from the baby when doing this movement, this means that the baby does not fully understand this sensation. It makes the need for this activity even more important. Always be very gentle and never force the movement. For the first few days, make the movements small and brief. As you continue these movements, the baby will begin to understand them more, and they will get easier. Repeat the movements for about 15 seconds on each hand, or about 15 to 20 movements.

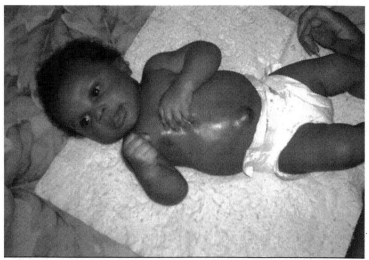

This four-month-old girl is doing the tummy rub with her mom. She is demonstrating that her hand is able to stay open and the palm of her hand is in contact with her tummy.

Leg Rub

Using the lubricant, now gently rub some of the lubricant on the insides of the baby's thighs, knees, lower legs, and ankles. Hold one of the baby's legs in each of your hands and gently rub them together, with the legs bent, so that as much of his skin contacts the other leg's skin as possible. Do this for a repetition of about 20 movements. The movement should be done fairly slowly. Again, if there is resistance to the movement, do not force it. Be very gentle and do only what the baby allows. With repetition the movement should become very smooth.

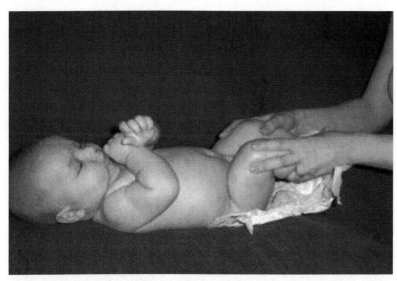

This three-month-old boy and his mother are demonstrating the leg rub. Note the contact surfaces of the inside of the legs and ankles are being rubbed against each other with lubrication. This technique is done with light rubbing.

Suggestion for Busy Parents

Doing the tummy-leg rub is easiest at diaper changes. Both the arms and legs should only take about two minutes at the most. If the lubricant is kept at the diaper changing station, this activity fits easily into a busy schedule.

Chapter 8

Carrying Baby

The way babies are carried has changed significantly over the past 25 years. Plastic is "in" and human touch is "out". Car seats are critical. There is no question that babies must be in an approved infant seat while riding in a motor vehicle. This discussion does not pertain to that. Rather, this discussion is about keeping babies in plastic carriers to transport them everywhere else. Not only are babies transported in plastic seats, many babies sleep in them and spend much time awake in them. For entertainment, the baby is often placed in a hard plastic seat such as a swing, jumper, or ExerSaucer®. The author refers to this phenomenon as "container babies".

Research is just starting to address the effects baby equipment has on development. There is not much data on long term effects or how this equipment may be impacting systems other than the motor system. There have been a few studies that suggest that the more time a baby spends in containers, the lower the score on motor development tests and conversely the less time spent in containers, the higher the score on motor development tests.[51, 64] At this time it appears that perhaps this delay does not persist into later stages of childhood, but remembering the importance of foundation building, why would a parent create an environment that may cause a less sturdy foundation? Limiting the time a baby spends in a container is a great way to build a sturdy foundation!

Often, once the parents have carried their baby to their destination, they leave the baby in the infant seat for sleeping and awake time. Parents are even using infant seats for a positioning device in the home. Time spent in an infant seat is "zero developmental time." This means that there is no appropriate sensory input happening during this time. And even worse, for babies spending much time in containers they miss out on valuable floor time where they will learn to hold their head up, roll and sit up. A third disadvantage of too much time spent in a container is developing a flat spot on the skull, plagiocephaly. Skulls that become misshapen from too much time spent in a container may have a more severe deformity than one that is from a congenital condition (occurs in the womb). [9]

There is a vast difference between carrying a baby in the arms of his dad or mom versus carrying a baby in a plastic infant seat. While baby is carried in human arms and possibly over the shoulder, he feels the warmth and security of another person's body. As the person walks, the baby's sensory system gets feedback from that person's muscles, and the baby makes his own adjustments accordingly. When being held over the shoulder, the baby works on important neck and back muscles as he tries to hold his head up. He is even more challenged in his motor skills when the person holding him over the shoulder begins to walk. During this activity, there is good support for the baby's spine as the person holds the baby's back. When he is held in front of a person's body, the baby may snuggle into the person's chest and hear that person's heartbeat, smell dad or mom's familiar smell, and get important skin-to-skin contact. The gentle changes in pressure that are involved when a baby is carried in their parent's arms instead of in plastic help develop the baby's touch and muscle system. These experiences help build the sensory-motor foundation.

The baby being carried in a plastic infant carrier has a different experience. The baby's body is slanted in an upright position at a period in development before his muscles can support his spine. Usually, the baby's posture falls to the side, curving his spine sideways. While in this plastic seat, there is no human warmth or muscle feedback from another person's body. Instead of feeling the smooth movements of his parent, the baby often has a ride in a plastic carrier that is bumpy and jarring. The primary stimulation is visual, since little muscular effort is needed on the baby's part, and he is in a position to be visually stimulated. As previously stated, during the ages of birth to six months, the focus needs to be on the more basic systems of touch, muscle sensation, and movement coordination, rather than the higher sensory system of vision. By using infant seats to transport the baby, the baby is deprived of many of the sensations that he needs most at this time, and he is encouraged to turn on his visual system, which is a higher level system.

 ### *Reinforce previous sensory-motor experiences.*
Baby slings made of fabric that hold a baby in a flexed position next to dad or mom's chest work well to reinforce the fetal position and at the same time allow baby to be close to their parent's heartbeat as well as their smell. Slings that have a padded shoulder for the parent's comfort and do not have tight elastic at the edges are preferred. It has been this author's experience that the sooner after birth that the sling is used, the more easily a baby will adapt to it and actually love it. A suggestion to make the sling more successful is to have mom wear the sling a few times before baby arrives. In doing this, the sling will have mom's scent on it. The first time baby is in the sling he will experience a familiar smell and will adapt to this new position (which is similar to the one in the womb!) with greater ease.

Another style of cloth baby carriers puts the baby's legs in a spread apart position. Although this way of carrying a baby is better than the plastic carrier, it is not as good as the sling. The sling reinforces the fetal flexion position. The sling is a key to building a better foundation!

This three-month-old boy is being carried by his mother. Note how he is working to hold his head up. Also note the skin-to-skin contact with his mother. His muscle system is actively involved while using his visual system.

Here is an example of a mother using a sling carrier for her child. Note that the child is curled in the fetal flexed position and is experiencing closeness to his mother. His spine is totally supported and he is receiving valuable gentle pressure around his body from the sling. Plain colored fabric is best for the times baby is nestled into the sling. The plain color prevents visual distractions at near-point vision.

There are babies who would rather be carried in an infant seat. These may be babies who do not generally like to be held or to be in the fetal flexion position. Even though they may fuss or arch backwards while in either of these positions, they really need to be held and to be in the fetal flexion position. They may be having difficulty understanding or organizing the systems of touch, muscle tone, or body posture in flexion. They try to "skip" some of these more calming and basic foundational activities and are mainly content with visual stimulation. In order to build a solid foundation for these babies, it is essential that they have frequent, short intervals of holding, cuddling, and being in a flexed position. When they gain more experience in these positions, they will understand the sensations and be more comfortable. During the ages of birth to six months, human touch, holding, and cuddling are as important as the nutrition they receive. The blocks of a baby's sensory-motor foundation are more solid if he receives essential human touch.

> Our oldest son, Blake, did not initially like to be held as an infant. He was born in Korea and arrived "home" at age four months. During one of our baby showers two women almost dropped him. I have pictures of him arching backward out of people's arms. He was strong and determined! Using the keys in this book, within a few months he began to love being held and snuggled. I felt so strongly about the negative effects of plastic infant carriers that we never owned one for any of our children.

From a developmental standpoint, the preferred methods of carrying a baby are to simply hold and cuddle him or to use a sling system that fits over the parent's shoulder. By utilizing these carrying techniques rather than the plastic infant seat, the baby is building a more solid foundation for development and learning.

Chapter 9

Bathtub Activity

The bathtub activity can be used to calm a fussy baby or just for the sheer enjoyment it brings to the parent and the way that it enriches the parent-infant bond. This activity also enhances many basic developmental areas, such as touch and muscle tone. The skin-to-skin contact of the parent and child has been shown to have a positive impact on the child's perceptual-cognitive and motor development.[55]

Fill the bathtub with warm (body temperature: 98° to 99° F) water. A pool thermometer can be used to ensure proper temperature. The bathroom light should be turned off and the hall light left on, with the bathroom door ajar. This produces a dimly lit room. The baby is then taken into the tub with the parent. The baby should be in flexion (curled up) on the chest, with the baby's back against the parent's chest.

Reinforce previous sensory-motor experiences.
The bathtub activity can be used to do any number of gentle, calming activities. One may gently sway the baby from side to side while held in flexion, in the position suggested above. The baby will feel the water lightly flow over his skin, which

is a familiar sensation from the womb. The parent can then gently massage the baby's arms, legs, and back. Another excellent activity is for the parent to rub the baby's hand on his tummy and rub his legs together, like in the tummy-leg rub activity in Chapter 7. Because the water provides the lubrication, no oil or lotion is needed in the bathtub. Several mothers have found that their babies nurse better during this activity because of the warmth and skin to skin contact, especially babies who are having difficulty with latching.

When the water begins to cool, most babies will begin to fuss. The length of time with this activity is not important. It is the experience that counts.

This activity is often an effective tool to enhance relaxation and promote parent-child bonding. It can be done as soon after birth as the doctor allows a baby to be in water. The baby is familiar with most of the sensory elements in this activity. One should not be discouraged if it takes 15 minutes to get the tub and baby ready and the activity only lasts 5 to 10 minutes. Because the baby is familiar with most of the sensory elements in this activity, the positive impact of 5 to 10 minutes in the tub is extremely powerful. The preparation time is worth it!

> A therapist who is a friend of mine is a big advocate of this bathtub activity. She has many examples of this activity being instrumental in building a sensory-motor foundation. One such child, Keith, was eight months old. He did not tolerate being on his tummy on the floor and did not enjoy being held. After three sessions in the bathtub with his mother his system began to change. He now enjoyed being on his tummy and being held. The bathtub activity helped to fill in the sensory-motor information that was incomplete in the blocks of his foundation. This more solid foundation allowed the higher skills of cuddling and

being on his tummy to function better. He was ready to move and be less irritable!

Demonstration of positioning for the bathtub activity.

Chapter 10

Massage and Deep Pressure

There are many massage books on the market for use with babies. Massage is any systematic application of touch; it has proven to be a valuable tool for babies. Massage has been shown to help with weight gain, sleep-wake patterns, the ability to calm, bone strength and motor development. Skin to skin contact is critical for the development of a child. Holding, cuddling, bathing, and massage are all ways to accomplish this. Most massage techniques are gentle and provide smooth skin stimulation. This is appropriate for the very young baby.

Starting at about one month of age, another massage technique, called deep pressure is very powerful. It differs from other massage techniques because it affects the muscle more than the skin and stimulates sensations a bit deeper. Deep pressure is done by using your thumb and gently pushing into the baby's muscle until the bone is felt underneath. The sensation of deep pressure is a critical sensory function that is a foundation for coordinated movement. This technique is known to be a normalizer. It can decrease high muscle tone (tight muscles) and increase low muscle tone (loose muscles). It also improves muscle sensation and, thereby, improves muscle function.

Do deep pressure in a quiet, relaxed atmosphere with few visual distractions. It works well if the baby is held in the adult's lap, but it can also be done with a baby lying on his tummy. The illustrations on pages 56 and 57 show the areas where to apply deep pressure.

The exact spots are not critical, and it does not matter where it is started. Deep pressure is not done on the abdomen because of the internal organs under the abdominal wall. The biceps and calves are also avoided as they seem to be very sensitive to deep pressure and may respond with an increased muscle tone response instead of a normalized response.

The thumb is used to press into the areas shown on these illustrations. Only enough pressure is applied to go through the muscle to gently touch the bony area—the less muscle, the less pressure. It is important to apply enough pressure to touch the bone as this is the area that has the receptors to process deep pressure. Babies tolerate this much better if moving from point to point is done slowly. If a baby cries, try doing only one area at a time. Deep pressure is usually tolerated better on the arms than on the legs. By proceeding slowly a baby will soon tolerate deep pressure on his entire body. The ideal response from deep pressure is to get a contraction of the muscle through which the pressure is being applied. Before the body fully understands this stimulation, the child may respond in a variety of ways. The child may perceive deep pressure as ticklish, painful, pleasurable or not at all. Many muscles may contract instead of the one being stimulated. These responses are often seen before the body processes the stimulation correctly.

Each baby tolerates deep pressure based on his understanding of previous sensory experiences. In other words, if the foundation block from a prenatal experience is not filled in completely it may cause a lack of total understanding of the sensation of deep pressure. This could cause the sensation to be "irritating". The goal for the baby is to tolerate deep pressure without a great deal of stress. If a baby fusses but stops right after deep pressure is stopped, that level of stress is acceptable. If deep pressure sends a baby into a five-minute crying fit, then try doing only one body part, such as the palms of the hands, and do a different body part at another time. Eventually a tolerance will be built up. This process is extremely helpful. Building up a tolerance to deep pressure means that the body begins to understand that sensation and it is not irritable.

Deep pressure is one of the most valuable tools and it should be done at least one time per day. Deep pressure cannot be done too often, so more than once per day is fine. Some literature suggests three times daily to be ideal. The effects of deep pressure seem to last at least 20 minutes, so it is helpful to do deep pressure prior to the baby working on motor skills such as being on tummy, crawling, and creeping. Once deep pressure is mastered by the person doing it, the time involved should be less than two minutes. When deep pressure provides an increased sense of calm and awareness about the body . . . a foundation block is filled in!

I have found that the majority of children come to love deep pressure. In fact, I cannot honestly think of one child who has not come to tolerate it when we have been slow and consistent with the technique. I have experienced many toddlers and older children who ask for deep pressure. They understand that deep pressure helps them calm down, focus, and have a sense of well-being.

Deep Pressure Instructions

1. Press into the palm of the hand (not the fingers). Do the edges of the palm in a circle and then do one point in the middle.

2. On the forearm, start at the wrist and work towards the elbow. Do the same thing on the under side of the forearm.

3. Start on the back of the arm just above the elbow. Press until just below the shoulder. Work on the outside of the arm; do not do the inside.

4. Repeat #1, #2 and #3 on the other arm.

5. Begin at the base of the neck on one side of the vertebral column (spine) and move downwards until you reach the sacrum (solid bone near end); at that point move outward towards the hip on that side. Repeat, starting on the other side. Remember to stay on the most muscular part and not on the bony area.

6. Start just below the hip on the outside of the leg and progress down to the knee.

7. Just above the back of the knee are two tendons. Start just above one of the dimples on the back of the knee. Move upward into the middle of the buttock area (cross the hip). Do the same above the other dimple.

8. Start in front of the hip and move down to just above the knee.

9. Press into the sole of the foot (not the toes). Do the edges of the sole in a circle and then up the middle.

10. Repeat #6, #7, #8 and #9 on the other leg.

Chapter 11

Activities to Avoid

"Container" Baby

One must avoid the use of containers whenever possible. If a container is necessary, limit the time spent in the container. Containers include infant carriers, Bumbo® seats, swings and ExerSaucers®. The Bumbo® seat has become popular recently. The concerns for using this seat are that it promotes a round neck and back posture and that baby is not actively using back muscles in a way that is developmentally appropriate. The time spent in a Bumbo® is time the baby cannot explore his environment. Despite the negative impacts these containers have on development, most babies spend more time in these than they do on the floor or being held. Sitting should not be an activity of choice until a baby gets into sitting by himself. The spine is not supported well by muscles at this stage, and the position of the back being curved may cause some future back problems. Also, the sitting position stimulates the visual system which should not be emphasized in early infancy. Finally, excess use of containers may contribute to plagiocephaly (misshapen skull).

Music and Noise

Music and noise should not be a constant for a baby. He needs quiet time at various times throughout the day. At this age, babies are generally overly stimulated and need help to be in an environment that encourages calm, relaxed function.

Visual Stimulation in Crib

Parents should not place visually stimulating items in the crib, such as mirrors or mobiles. The crib should be a place where baby calms, sleeps and moves.

Hanging Toys near Baby's Face

One should avoid toys that hang near a baby's face. Parents should encourage the use of vision at a distance rather than up close. During the stage of birth to six months, vision should not be a system that is overly stimulated. Toys that hang so that baby can bat at them are encouraging the use of the visual system in a way that is too high of a skill for this developmental time frame.

Chapter 12

Summary
Early Infancy—Birth through Six Months

Building Babies Better by developing a solid foundation is exciting! At this point it may seem a bit more overwhelming than exciting. The following summary of recommendations is provided in hopes of making this building process easier:

Crib Time

- Use plain crib sheets and bumper pads.
- Do not place mobiles or mirrors in the crib.
- Provide the sound of the heartbeat occasionally during times of rest.
- Avoid the use of classical music at this developmental stage.
- Allow periods of quiet everyday.
- Avoid utilizing a night-light in the baby's room that is left on all night.
- Provide rests in total darkness.

Tummy Time

Place a piece of heavy ply plastic or floor vinyl (minimum size 3'x3' with as little texture and visual detail as possible) on the carpet for an "exercise" area for your baby. Create a "slick" environment by either dressing the baby in clothes that cover his arms and legs (keep feet bare) or put some oil on the unclothed baby and exercise surface. Place the baby on his tummy and let tummy time begin!

Diaper Changes

Keep lotion or oil at the diaper changing station so that the tummy-leg rub activity can be done several times per day.

Carrying Baby

- Avoid using plastic infant carriers whenever possible.
- Hold a baby in various positions when carrying him, such as on the parent's shoulder, cuddled in front of the parent, or in a cloth, over-the-shoulder, "sling" carrier.
- When holding and feeding a baby with a bottle, alternate holding him with his head resting in your right or left arm to give him equal experience on both sides.
- Enjoy eye-to-eye contact with baby.

Bathtub

With the bathroom dimly lit and the tub filled with body temperature water (98°-99° F), with both you and the baby in the tub, hold the baby close for skin-to-skin contact and gently swish water over the baby's body.

Deep Pressure Massage

Do deep pressure massage at least once per day to help baby calm and use his muscles more effectively during activity.

Part II

Older Baby
Six Months through Beginning to Walk

This is an especially exciting time to watch a baby develop, refine, and repeat motor skills. During this stage, a baby will accomplish belly crawling for locomotion, sitting, creeping on hands and knees, pulling to stand, cruise walking holding onto furniture, and finally walking. Amazingly, he usually does all of this in a six to eight month time frame! The bursting of new developmental skills will never again be so obvious.

In this author's physical therapy practice, one of the most frequently asked questions has been, "When should my baby begin walking?" In terms of "norm" age, studies show that this can be anywhere from 11 months to 15 months. Many babies walk earlier than this and a few walk later. In a society that showcases any extraordinary expression of skill and tends to honor only the brightest and the best, parents have come to be very proud of the age at which their babies learn to walk, especially if it is an early age. Many parents say, "I didn't push my child into walking early. He just did it on his own." This is true in some cases. Some babies are genetically accelerated to walk early. It is the finding of this therapist that the majority of early walkers were babies that did not get much tummy time and spent much of their time upright in infant seats, ExerSaucers® and swings. They also were in an environment that encouraged pulling to standing and walking behind toys.

After studying development for over 30 years, this author has concluded that there is a definite purpose in the way that our development was designed. Skipping or accelerating stages may eventually lead to a weakness or failure in the system. Give or take a few months, a child has one precious year in which he can work on sensory-motor skills from a prone (on the tummy) or hands and knees position. These positions build up strength and coordination in the shoulders, back and hips in ways that cannot be built up in the upright position. Once the child is upright, his whole perspective on the world changes. Although the goal is for a child to be upright and develop the best possible high-level skills, it is detrimental to facilitate early upright posture or walking. If the child is not ready to be upright or walking on his own, he needs more time to build background information.

> One day I was having a conversation with a new acquaintance of mine. We began discussing child development issues. I expressed that I felt it was better if children walked later rather than earlier and outlined the benefits of pre-walking skills. At this point, this woman started to cry and said that I had just given her a gift. She explained that her son, Michael, who was now five years old, had not started to walk independently by the time he was 15 months old. Although her doctor assured her that everything was fine, her well-meaning friends kept reinforcing how young their children were when they learned to walk and questioning whether something was wrong with her son. Even though her son was a precocious five year old who was doing great, the strong emotions of that worrisome time welled up within her. What a relief for her to discover that it was a good thing that Michael had waited to walk!

Experience has shown that even if a child is not ready to walk, he can still be taught to walk. Activities that will teach your baby to walk too early include: baby walkers, ExerSaucers®, play pens, toys to stand behind and push, jump-up types of sling seats where the baby's feet touch the floor, and, finally, an adult physically putting the baby on his feet and helping him to take steps. If the goal for a child is to have the best developmental background, it is important not to "teach" the baby to walk. Watching a baby become proficient in crawling (on belly) and creeping (on hands and knees) is superior to being in the race for a child to be an early walker. A parent should be proud of the hard work that a baby does on the floor, knowing that he will never have this type of opportunity again. When a baby does begin to walk independently on his own time schedule, the quality of his walking is better and more coordinated than if he is "taught" to walk earlier . . . less bumps, bruises, and skinned knees!

Another consideration relating to this topic is "genetically accelerated" babies. These are babies who walk early, and there is nothing that one can do to slow them down. From the moment they are born, they are more alert and driven to be upright. They are especially in need of calming activities. One should encourage them to slow down and experience crawling and creeping. It may be difficult to slow these babies down, but certainly it is imperative not to push them to develop faster. They already have the internal program to go faster and they need a balance. Parents should keep in mind that having a complete background of sensory-motor skills is the goal, not rushing through these early skills to be the first to the finish line.

Chapter 13

Play Time While on Tummy on Slick Surface

Being on the floor on his tummy is the best place for the baby to develop strength and coordination of back and shoulder muscles. The smooth surface that was described in chapter 6 continues to be appropriate for this age. When a baby has reached the stage that he is belly crawling across the floor, there is no need to do the oil activity. Just being on a wood floor, vinyl flooring over carpet, or the plastic with clothes covering the belly and legs will create less resistance to movement. This surface is appropriate until baby gets up on his hands and knees. When a baby is no longer belly crawling, a smooth surface is not needed. When encouraging a baby to crawl on his belly it is best to put just one or two toys at a time on the floor for motivation. It is important not to overload his visual field with many toys. Pivoting while on the tummy is an activity babies do before they crawl. It is important to place a toy off to the side to encourage baby to pivot to the side. One should repeat this to each side to develop skills on both sides of the body. The following are some additional activities that are especially beneficial when a baby is on his tummy:

Blocks

Parents or older siblings may stack blocks and encourage a baby to knock them over. Large blocks without much visual detail are best. Blocks that make a gentle noise when they are knocked over are more interesting. There are also cloth blocks with bells inside that work well.

Open-Hand Pounding

Providing a toy that requires a baby to pat it to produce a gentle sound or light reinforces good palm sensations. The background for this activity was the tummy-hand rub from chapter 7. By stimulating the sensory receptors in the palm of the hand, the sensory-motor foundation will be built for later use of the fingers. Offering this toy to both sides so that baby learns to shift weight onto each side and use each hand encourages activities that use both sides of the body. There should be no hand preference at this stage of development.

Pie tins and plastic bowls are great for pounding. Some commercial toys produce too loud of a sound and are overly stimulating (for parents, too!). Putting tape over the speaker of the toy will help to lessen the sound. Another good toy for this activity is a pat-mat. This is a mat that is filled with a fluid or squishy material and has floating objects that move when the mat is patted. This play activity should be done with a baby on his tummy or held supported in a parent's lap. If a baby can get into sitting by himself, then sitting on the floor is another good position.

Large Ball

This is a good age to obtain a large ball (12 inches in diameter or larger) that is one color without detail on the ball. A larger ball is better than a smaller ball because it requires more big muscle activity. The large ball provides a great activity when a baby is on the floor. Even before a baby begins to crawl, he can learn to explore and develop useful motor skills. By putting the ball on the floor next to a wall, preferably in a corner, and placing a baby on the floor next to the ball, baby will begin to interact with the ball. While on his tummy he can begin to explore the ball by himself. He will begin to push the ball with an open hand. Because the ball is against the wall, it will come back to him. He may roll over onto his back and begin to play the same game with his feet. Once a baby begins to crawl, he will enjoy pushing the ball and chasing it.

Moving Hands and Legs on Slick Surface

In the stage before a baby has figured out how to move about on his tummy, this exercise is helpful. It is especially important for those babies who like to keep their legs off the surface in an "airplane" posture, and it will provide sensory feedback that will enhance good movement.

With a baby on his tummy on the smooth surface, move his hand up and down along the surface. Do this one side at a time. It is good to repeat this about ten times. This will provide a baby with the sensation of what it will be like for him to move his arm properly in crawling. Also, if his head is turned in the direction of the moving hand, this activity can help in the development of eye/hand coordination. Next, move each leg through a crawl motion about ten times each. The crawl motion for the leg is the knee bending and moving upward toward the shoulder. It is important for the arm and leg to stay in contact with the slick surface. This provides the baby with the sensory feedback to develop good coordination. It only takes one minute to do this exercise. Often a baby will then repeat the movements on his own. (See picture in chapter 6 for demonstration of crawl motions of the leg.) This activity can be done either in oil or with long sleeves and long pants. Either way it is important the surface be smooth, such as plastic or vinyl.

Chapter 14

Smooth Surface for Belly Crawling

Chapter 6 discusses the concept of a smooth surface on which to place a baby on the floor. This environment continues to be appropriate until a baby masters belly crawling and begins creeping on hands and knees. Carpeting provides more surface friction for belly crawling. When a baby is on a smooth surface, the sensation on the skin during movements is more enjoyable while the effort required is less. Many children will not belly crawl if placed only on carpeted surfaces or blankets, so it is important to provide either a vinyl or wood floor. If the area where a baby plays is carpeted, lay a large sheet of floor vinyl over the carpet temporarily until he begins creeping on hands and knees. Once a baby begins creeping on hands and knees, there is still an advantage to a smooth surface. The smooth surface will encourage the hand to be open and in some cases the carpet encourages the hand to be closed. During creeping on hands and knees the baby is everywhere, so providing both surfaces is appropriate.

In preparing the floor surface where a baby learns to belly crawl, the area should be fairly large as most babies like to really move on the smooth surface. The area should be at least 6' x 9'. The cost of a piece of vinyl flooring is relatively inexpensive—about the same price as one of those light-up, singing toys that over-stimulates a baby at this stage! The heavy ply plastic used for the tummy time activity is a small space for crawling, but is preferred to carpet.

The larger wood or vinyl space encourages movement across larger spaces.

One should be sure to have only one or two toys down on the floor by the baby, placing the toys just out of reach so that he has an incentive to move. Parents should not clutter the play space with toys. If it is cluttered, there is less space to move. When there is too much to see, a baby is more entertained with the toys and has less motivation to move and explore.

A piece of vinyl flooring has been placed over the carpet to create a smooth surface. This surface is appropriate to develop good belly crawling.

A colleague called me one day asking for some help with his daughter, Jennifer, who was nine months old and was not yet crawling. He was concerned that her development was not normal. When I met his daughter and visited with both parents, I discovered that this was primarily an environmental problem rather than a problem with Jennifer's development. This baby girl was very "turned on" to the visual input and details of toys. She was able to sit up by herself, and the parents would put her on the floor and surround her with toys. She had a large number of toys and was constantly entertained by toy bars (bars that have various toys suspended from them), music boxes, and other stimulating items. There was very little clear space in which she could move and almost no motivation for her to do so. My suggestions were simple: deep pressure, create a slick surface and limit the number of toys. First I taught the parents deep pressure. Deep pressure would give Jennifer a better sense of her muscles and body. The parents obtained a piece of vinyl flooring to create a smooth crawl surface. We agreed they would put away all of her toys and rotate a few of them out at a time. When it was time for Jennifer to play, they would place one or two toys on the vinyl, just out of her reach. At first, this was a bit frustrating for Jennifer, but in about one week the parents called to let me know that she was crawling all over the place!

Chapter 15

Sitting

Allow baby to grow into higher skills.
The age range for sitting varies. Usually babies start getting into sitting by themselves between seven and ten months of age. Until a baby accomplishes this, the coordination of the neck and back muscles is not sufficient to support and hold the body upright. If a baby is continually placed in a sitting position, (either in a high chair, propped on a couch, or any other type of supported sitting,) a skill is encouraged that the baby is not yet ready to accomplish. This pediatric therapist is concerned when a baby is left in positions where the spine is curved for long periods of time. Although research has not yet been done to determine if sitting in containers for long periods of time has a negative impact on the spine, it does exist concerning baby's heads and it shows that it can have a negative impact on skull shape.[61]

Although sitting should be kept to a minimum until the baby can get into sitting by himself, there will be times when it is necessary. For example, a baby may need to sit in a high chair to eat before he begins sitting by himself. If so, parents should place the baby in the high chair only during the time that is necessary for feeding. Another time sitting is necessary is in a car seat. It helps to think of times when the baby is in a car seat as zero developmental time. This should motivate parents to keep errands to a minimum and the baby out of the car as much as possible.

The best time to encourage sitting for a baby is after he has learned to get into a sitting position by himself. By this time a baby can support an upright spine without the muscles fatiguing and the back curving forward. Current research shows that when a baby sits unsupported (not in a container and not propped on arms), the baby's rib cage is freed and the baby can breathe more deeply as well as use that breath more efficiently for speech production.[70] In addition, research has shown that the quality of an infant's reaching improves with increased development of postural stability in sitting.[69] In the time leading up to a baby sitting by himself, it is best for baby to either be held, placed on the floor on his tummy, or in a horizontal position in a swing or stroller.

> Recently I was given a reality check on this recommendation. I spent time in a daycare center! It is easy to understand why babies in daycare spend more time in containers than babies not in daycare. Certainly propping baby in a container or a Bumbo® chair entertains many babies. Working with the daycare staff, who absolutely wanted to do what was best for the baby, we came up with some changes to the environment to make it more positive. Once they understood some of the concepts in this book they realized they could limit time in containers by having less containers and more floor space. They had a wonderful mat in a solid color (better contrast for vision) for babies to lie on their tummy. If they did place a child in an ExerSaucer® or Bumbo® (yikes!) they tried to have that be a very temporary place, knowing it was best for the baby to be on the floor.

Understanding the basic principles of *Building Babies Better* allows anyone to make the best decisions possible for the environment in which the baby is developing. It is not always possible, nor is it necessary, to have a perfect developmental environment. It is critical to understand what a good developmental environment is so that the best decisions can be made.

*This eight-month-old infant is on his way
to good postural stability!
He has a very straight back and easily uses his hands
in play while sitting.*

Chapter 16

Fine Motor Skills

 Gross motor comes before fine motor.
Fine motor skills involve the use of fingers for activities such as picking up small pieces of food, turning pages in a book, and holding a writing utensil. Optimal use of these skills requires a strong base of gross motor skills. Without good shoulder control and trunk muscles to provide stabilization, a child may tire quickly, become frustrated or lose interest in fine motor activities. A poor gross motor foundation may also affect the quality of a child's fine motor skills. Therefore, this is the age to emphasize activities that encourage strength and coordination of trunk and shoulder muscles, rather than just the use of fingers. Efficiency in the gross motor skill of reaching emerges before the fine motor skill of precision grasp.[73]

There are many kinds of touch experiences that are perceived by the fingertips and palms. Sensations in the palms are a foundation skill for sensations of the fingertips. At this stage of development it is important to provide activities to enhance palm sensations.

Understanding these experiences fills another foundational block needed for fine motor skills. The following are a few examples of fun activities to meet these goals.

Encourage activities that use both sides of the body.

This 12-month-old boy is demonstrating a great play activity that requires using both arms together and works on shoulder muscles. Playing with this large ball is preparing him to have good use of his fine motor skills when he is older.

Large Toys

Parents should provide toys that require both hands to pick them up (e.g., large balls or large blocks). One should be sure the balls are properly inflated or some children will pinch the ball and still only use one hand. Large blocks can be made by covering shoeboxes with contact paper. Sometimes an older baby will enjoy playing with a large empty box that he will pick up with two hands. Instead of smaller trucks and cars, one should provide the large ones. These require more shoulder function as well as the use of gross motor skills while pushing.

Batting/Banging Activities

It is important to encourage activities that involve batting at objects with an open hand (e.g., a suspended ball, splashing in the tub, or hitting a pie tin or drum). By providing activities that require an open hand, palm sensations will be enhanced. Having baby hold a block in each hand and bang them together also works on shoulder muscles. Provide blocks that are bigger and require an open hand to hold.

Palm Painting

A fun activity is "palm painting". To "palm paint", a parent places pudding, yogurt, vegetable oil, or any slippery, edible substance on the tray of the high chair. Baby smears the "paint" with an open hand so that most of the work is being done by his shoulder muscles. The parent should encourage big circles or lines side to side by gently placing her hand over the baby's hand for a few minutes and gliding his hand in different directions. Then the parent removes his hand and let's the baby do his own thing. This activity enhances sensory functions in the palm of the hand.

Some ways babies under the age of one work on appropriate fine motor skills include: grasping at toys (three to four months); playing with their toes while lying on their backs (six to seven months); and waving "bye-bye" (nine to ten months). More precise fine motor activities such as picking up small bits of food on the tray using a pincer grasp, is appropriate around 12 months of age.

In summary, the best fine motor skill development allows for time to develop a good base of control in the shoulders, hips and back before precise use of the fingers is emphasized. At this age, providing toys that encourage the sensations of the palms as well as the use of two hands is the best way to build a foundation for great fine motor skills.

Chapter 17

Platform Activity

This seven-month-old boy is enjoying climbing on and off this box. His shoulders are taking more weight as he climbs off the box. This prepares him for being on his hands and knees in creeping.

Once a baby is belly crawling, this platform activity helps him develop better motor planning and reinforces good sensory input, especially in the shoulders. Motor planning is when, by trial and error, a baby learns to move his body in ways that will accomplish his task.

One of my little friends, Jill, taught me a great deal about using a platform. She had just learned to crawl on her tummy. I suggested that Mom get a platform, and she located a box about 3 inches high, 24 inches deep, and 30 inches wide. Mom created a wonderful environment for crawling by placing a large piece of vinyl flooring over their carpet and then setting the box in the middle of it. At first, Mom put Jill's favorite toy on top of the box to motivate her to explore the higher surface. Soon Jill learned to climb on and off the box and she no longer needed an incentive to climb. She enjoyed climbing just for the motor fun of it, and she was so proud of her accomplishment! Next we found a higher surface for Jill and discovered that she could begin to get into a sitting position by climbing onto the box with her arms and trunk, and then lowering her hips to the floor. Watching Jill learn about her body while she explored this platform was a joy!

The platform activity is done by putting a platform in the middle of the floor onto which the baby crawls. Start with a platform about two to three inches high and large enough to fit a baby's entire body. The edges should be rounded so that a baby cannot hurt himself. Tops to large plastic storage boxes and pizza boxes will work well for this. Walking around the house and looking for the right item often turns up the perfect platform. Wrapping the platform in a blanket can make the surface softer in case of a bump or fall, but try to keep the friction for crawling onto and off of the platform to a minimum.

After a baby can easily crawl up on a low platform, he is ready for something a bit higher (e.g., six to eight inches). For this activity, it is best to let a baby learn all about the platform on his own. In the beginning, a favorite toy on top of the platform can be used to provide incentive for a baby to climb on top, as in Jill's case. Eventually, a baby needs to figure out how to get up and down on his own. This is what motor planning is all about.

It is best if a baby enjoys climbing up and down just for the motor planning, not for getting a toy. Climbing down begins to develop good shoulder muscles, as the baby bears weight on his arms and gets him ready for creeping on hands and knees, as well.

The best environment for this activity is an uncluttered floor with no television on in the room. The crawling surface should be as described earlier, a slick surface of wood or vinyl. The platform should get progressively higher as the baby can handle the challenge. A baby's creative motor play on this platform is amazing! The only ingredient for this foundation building activity is a box on a slick surface.

Chapter 18

Play While Creeping on Hands and Knees

Once a baby is creeping on hands and knees, the proper floor surface can be carpet, vinyl, or wood. Creeping generally starts between seven and eleven months of age. The reason for the surface change is that the cushion effect of the carpet or rug makes being on the knees more comfortable. Many babies tolerate hard surfaces while on hands and knees quite well, also. Once a baby begins creeping on hands and knees exclusively, there is no need to encourage being only on a smooth surface. It is desirable for creeping to be done with the hand open and fingers extended. This enhances important sensations in the palm of the hand. If a baby tends to close his hand while creeping on carpet and opens his hand while creeping on a vinyl or wood surface, then it is helpful for the baby to spend time creeping on vinyl or wood to enhance the sensations of his palm.

This is another great time for the use of a large ball, which a baby can bat and chase. Being creative with space is important at this age. Open spaces in which a baby can move are critical at this time. Often a baby's space is cluttered with so many toys that he sits and uses his hands with toys most of the time. This is an age when he should be doing gross motor skills, such as creeping, batting at objects, and learning how to balance.

A clutter-free play space with occasional challenges to a baby's movement is ideal. For example, a cardboard box with two ends cut out placed on the floor for a baby to crawl through adds challenge and encourages gross motor activity. This is a wonderful motor experience upon which to later build the language concepts of "under" and "through". Tunnels can also be made using a blanket over two chairs or a coffee table. Play tunnels are available commercially. Another activity is to put several pillows or cushions from the couch on the floor for a baby to maneuver over and around. Inclines are great for learning to climb up and down. An incline can be made simply by putting a pillow under one end of a cushion that is already on the floor. Some families have even made various platforms and inclines out of plywood and then covered them with foam and vinyl cloth to make them safe in the event that baby falls on them. Small toddler slides are good for climbing up on hands and knees. Discovering new ways to go up and down the slide is great for motor planning, building core trunk strength, and so many other foundation building skills.

The developmental stage of creeping on hands and knees helps to fine tune the development of distance vision. The baby has important sensory feedback coming in from his palms at the same time that his eyes are at precisely the distance of his extended arm. This visual and touch sensory connection helps later eye-hand function. Creeping is also important in the development of depth perception as baby is now using vision with self movement up off of the floor. In addition to the importance of visual development there exist characteristics of the movement patterns of creeping on hands and knees that provide the background for coordinated walking. Certainly this stage of creeping on hands and knees is important to foundation building in many ways. There is no need to rush a child into walking. A child will be walking the majority of his life and he only has a few months to be creeping on hands and knees. Never again will the shoulder muscles be needed for locomotion. What a great stage to enhance and enjoy!

Chapter 19

Activities to Avoid

Early Standing

Allow baby to grow into higher skills.
One should not encourage standing until a child does it all by himself. This includes providing push toys before they are ready to walk. It is far better developmentally if a baby pulls to stand and takes steps independently when he is ready. The body is designed to "cruise walk" sideways holding onto furniture before walking forward. This "cruise walking" helps build muscles on the side of the hips, which are essential to good standing stability. If a baby does not walk until 13 to 15 months of age, he will have much vital time to experience and develop skills in crawling and creeping. It is essential to not try to accelerate this timetable for a baby.

Walkers/ExerSaucers®

Baby walkers and ExerSaucers® should not be used with a child of any age. They encourage a baby to be upright on his feet long before his developmental system is ready. They also encourage a baby to be visually attentive to his environment, but not in a way that is connected or coordinated with his body. Injuries and even death have been associated with walker use. The American Academy of Pediatrics has a policy statement recommending a ban on the manufacture and use of walkers due to the fact they have no positive impact on development and pose a serious threat to a baby's safety. [76] Babies using walkers demonstrate incorrect postures that encourage muscles to move in the wrong order.

Many people feel the ExerSaucers®is a good alternative, since it is stationary and the safety concerns are less. The ExerSaucers® does not provide a good developmental environment for a baby. While suspended in the bucket seat, baby may keep legs bent or stand stiff legged on their toes, neither of which fosters proper body alignment. The baby relies on the saucer for stability instead of using his back and abdominal muscles. The ExerSaucers® encourages weight bearing on the inside of the foot which can lead to foot deformities. No study has shown any benefits in the use of an ExerSaucers®. Professionals in the area of physical therapy have seen that babies spending considerable time in an ExerSaucers® display a decreased drive to explore and get from one place to another when they are out of the ExerSaucers®. [77]

"Jump Up" Seats

The use of suspended sling-type seats that allow a baby to be upright and jumping should always be avoided. Although they may be exercising leg muscles, the "jump up" seats are usually used at an age prior to a baby being able to walk by himself. Jumping comes long after the skill of walking and certainly not before it. Many babies are placed in these types of seats before they can sit independently, which is even worse. There is also concern of a "whiplash" type of injury since some babies can produce fast movement before their neck and trunk muscles can stabilize. The weight bearing on the foot is not correct and may encourage later foot deformities. Babies need to be down on the floor crawling on the belly or creeping on hands and knees for good development.

"Container" Baby

The importance of limiting the use of containers for babies may be reviewed in Chapter 11. Any time a baby is placed in a container in prop sitting, the exploration of his environment is limited to auditory and visual input. This is a time developmentally when baby needs to be moving. Locomotion and the development of locomotor skills are beneficial to all other areas of development. One should consider using a portable crib or other environment that will contain baby safely during those times it is necessary. This way, the baby is provided an environment that still allows him an opportunity to move and explore. If a container is necessary for safety reasons, the amount of time baby is in the container should be kept to a minimum. It is critical to remember that when a baby is in a container it is zero developmental time.

Television

The TV must be off! Many families leave their televisions on with either videos or TV programming as background noise. In some homes, the main time spent with a baby playing on the floor includes the TV on so the parent can "multi-task" during a favorite show. Although this may be an adequate environment for the parent, it is not a good developmental environment for the baby. Sensory images, both auditory and visual, enter our baby's nervous system whether they are paying attention to television or not. A baby's brain learns better if it is allowed to complete a task. When a baby is playing in a room that has the TV on, his attention to playing is interrupted with a bombardment of auditory noises and visual flashes. TV is meant to grab our attention. The visual images are rapid and the noise levels change on purpose. The advertisers do not want us to be in a room with their ad and not pay attention; they have studied nervous systems very well and do an excellent job of grabbing our attention. It is important to recognize that same "attention grabbing" is being done to our babies. Certainly there are times when the TV on in the room is important for other family members. The key here is to be sure the TV is off the majority of the time baby is playing.

Chapter 20

Summary
Older Baby—Six Months through Beginning to Walk

 ***Reinforce previous sensory-motor experiences.***
All of the activities described in the early infancy section can be used to reinforce good development.

Tummy Time Continues

Provide a smooth surface, such as wood or vinyl, on which a baby can learn belly crawling. Be sure there is space to move, with only one or two toys on the surface at a time.

Sitting

Avoid prop sitting or "containers", with the exception of being in a car seat for travel or in a high chair for feeding times. Once baby begins sitting on his own, all sitting activities can be done.

Fine Motor Activities

Provide large balls, toys at which to bat, toys to hit with an open hand, and toys that will encourage the use of both hands at once.

This is not an age to encourage use of fingers in activities such as drawing or picking up tiny objects. This is an age to develop great trunk and shoulder muscles so when a baby gets to be older he has a stable foundation to use fingers well. Gross motor skills are necessary for efficient, prolonged fine motor skills.

Platform Activity

Provide safe platforms of various heights on which baby can climb. The appropriate time to begin using platforms is when the baby begins belly crawling. Start with a platform with a height of about two inches and work higher as baby can handle the challenge. When a baby begins to creep on hands and knees platforms still provide good challenges.

Creeping on Hands and Knees

Continue to provide open spaces for baby to move through. Add interest and challenge to your baby's play space by using a cardboard box with two cut-out ends or design challenges with couch cushions.

Deep Pressure Massage

Continue deep pressure massage. Do this daily and more often if needed. Use deep pressure to calm a baby or alert his senses before doing motor activity. This activity will help to normalize muscle tone and give baby a better sense of body position.

Things to Avoid

- Walkers
- Exersaucers®
- Bumbo® seats
- "Jump Up" Seats
- Toys that encourage early standing and walking before a baby is doing these activities on his own
- Prop sitting or "containers" until a baby can get into sitting on his own
- TV/Videos

Part III

Special Issues

The six key principles outlined in *Building Babies Better* have many applications beyond the scope of babies from birth through one year. These include relating these concepts with older children and with children who have special needs. They also provide helpful insight into issues surrounding bonding and adoption.

These key principles continue to be effective beyond the age of one year. Up until the age of eight, the foundation skills continue to be a focus. Around the age of eight, the brain has reached a growth of about 95% of the volume of the adult size brain. Many developmental skills such as precise use of vision with moving objects and hand dominance have been established by the age of eight. After this age, most children become adept at more fine motor skills and their foundation allows for higher skills to come automatically. These six key principles are helpful in making a variety of decisions for your child through age eight such as: In what programs should my child participate? What toys are the best for my child? How do I provide for balance in my child's day?

Not only do these principles apply to children with normal development, but also to children with special needs. The majority of this author's work involves this group of children, and these key principles are used in designing physical therapy programs with all of them.

Another special issue for using these principles is in the area of bonding, both with birth and adopted children. Because there is a physical aspect to the bonding process, it is effective to utilize the sensory-motor activities outlined in this book.

It is not the intent of this author to provide a comprehensive look into the developmental needs of children beyond the age of one nor of children with special needs. Neither will all of the issues encompassed in the bonding process be considered. The purpose of this section, however, is to demonstrate how these key principles continue to be relevant regarding the sensory-motor needs of all children, regardless of their ages and situations.

Chapter 21

Beyond the Age of One

The first year of life is an explosion of change and development. Building a solid foundation is critical, but is the foundation complete in one year? No, it is not. All of the key principles still apply to development up until age eight. Before age eight, there continues to be a developmental emphasis on building the structure and foundation. Around age eight, the top of the pyramid is ready to take charge.

At this time, true developmental dominance is usually established. This developmental dominance differs from just hand dominance. Experts cannot agree on the age that hand dominance is established; the age range is from six months to eight years. One thing is for certain though; establishing dominance on one side of the brain is important and it is a process, not a point in time. There are many factors that are included in developmental dominance, not just handedness. These factors include emotional traits, visual functions, and cognitive functions. In a child with a good sensory motor foundation, the process of developmental dominance should be complete around the age of eight.

Toddler Foundations

At this stage of development, generally between fifteen months and three years, children really focus on gross motor skills. They are always on the move—exploring, tumbling, and climbing. Providing a safe, active environment in which they learn promotes a solid foundation. The following activities based on the key principles are appropriate at this age.

Reinforce previous sensory-motor experiences.

All of the activities outlined previously are still of benefit. When a toddler is seen crawling or creeping in play, this is good reinforcement of a previous skill. This is not a step backwards, but a time for foundation building. Deep pressure, holding in flexion, cuddling with skin contact and listening to the heartbeat continue to provide a calming environment. This is especially helpful for the active toddler. The cautions of having the play space be too cluttered with toys, sounds, or the television continue to hold at this age.

Encourage activities that use both sides of the body.

Two-handed activities consist of playing with large balls, using blocks the size of shoeboxes, and pushing toys that require both hands. Making the ball, block, or push toy heavier, which requires more muscle activity, enhances the benefits. This can be done by putting heavy objects in a push cart, placing heavier objects in a shoe box and taping it shut to use as a block, or finding heavier balls. One activity that is great for this age is to sit on the floor and roll a large ball back and forth between the child and a parent or older sibling. One should use a ball about the size of a playground ball so two hands are required. A ball that is one color and does not have designs on it is preferred. This is also a great activity for eye tracking. It encourages eye-hand coordination using big muscle work. Roll the ball side to side while you are in control of the ball to encourage the child to watch it before you roll it. Occasionally, the parent or sibling should roll the ball to the side of the child to encourage trunk rotation as he reaches for the ball.

This toddler is having a great time building with large blocks.
The large blocks require her to use both hands at once and also
get more of her body muscles involved in the activity. She is
squatting to play, which reinforces good flexion from
the previously learned flexion in the womb.

Gross motor comes before fine motor.

Parents should place the emphasis on gross motor activities rather than fine motor. As the toddler continues to grow, his body height and weight are in continual flux and, thus, so is his center of gravity. Working on gross motor activities facilitates the development of balance and the ability to control the center of gravity in a variety of tasks and environments. As postural control becomes more automatic, the toddler has more attention resources available for cognitive processing and learning higher level fine motor skills. This is an age where fine motor abilities are more apparent. The toddler can feed himself and use utensils to do so. While there are many toys that require pushing buttons or pointing a finger, both of which the toddler may be capable of doing, at this age, the emphasis should still be on big toys and lots of gross motor activities. When there is a choice between a gross motor activity and sitting down with small toys, the best choice is gross motor. Some great activities at this age include: playground activities, toddler slides, small climbing gyms, and jumping activities on small, safe trampoline type toys. Another consideration at this age is to use car and train mats on the floor rather than a table. Standing at a table playing requires less gross motor skill than being on hands and knees on the floor.

A toddler's television and video viewing should be kept to an absolute minimum. This activity is zero developmental time for a child this age. Electronic devices and computers are not appropriate for this age. Research has shown that although children through the age of three may be entertained by video (two dimensional stimulation), true learning is not taking place.[80] This is a time for experiential learning with the real world (three dimensional).

Allow baby to grow into higher skills.

Writing utensils at this age are not appropriate. This is not a time for precise, controlled fine motor activities. Instead of coloring or writing with a utensil, provide palm-finger painting. Foam soaps and bath tub paint are great for the sensory as well as the fine motor experience. Parents may spray the foam soap or bath tub paint into the child's hands and let him decorate the side of the tub or wash himself. Activities should be fun and creative with the focus on the process, not the product. This is a great age for the child to be a helper in activities that require big shoulder and hand movements. They love to help wash the car, clean windows, or wipe the table.

Preschool Foundations

Preschooler is a name that is almost out of date now. The majority of three—and four—year-old children today are in a school of some kind. We call these schools preschools, but many of them have taken on the characteristics of the kindergartens and even first grades of twenty years ago. To build a solid sensory-motor foundation, there still needs to be an emphasis on gross motor skills. Superior learning includes movement and touch experiences. This type of learning builds the foundation at the same time it teaches concepts.

Reinforce previous sensory-motor experiences.

Having "family exercise" sessions in the living room reinforces previous sensory-motor experiences. This will provide opportunities for some "rough" housing that includes much needed touch and skin contact. Belly crawling races across a smooth surface or creeping on hands and knees races across a carpeted surface will foundation build for both the adult and child! Children love when parents build an obstacle course of cushions, tunnels, and boxes. Climbing and outdoor play provides opportunity to reinforce skills from earlier ages.

Another area to reinforce is ball play. One of the foundational building activities to prepare for proficiency in ball play at a later stage is to spend lots of time playing with a larger ball which requires the use of two hands. A playground size ball is the best size ball to use until a child is five or six years of age. Catching a small ball is a skill that doesn't develop well until around age five. A child in the preschool years should spend lots of time outside throwing, catching, kicking and trying to bounce a big ball.

Avoid small, detailed visual images.

Appropriate fine motor activities for a preschooler encourage shoulder movement along with avoiding small, detailed visual images. Looking at small detailed images within arm's length is a skill for the top of the developmental pyramid. It is best at this age if the images are large and greater than arm's length in distance. Working vision at a close range for prolonged periods of time is associated with myopia (near sightedness in which distant objects are blurred). Research has found that when children are given adequate time to play outside (where vision is used at a distance) this has a protective effect on vision.[26]

At this age, it is important to pay attention to writing utensils. Precise marks are not important and should not be stressed at this age. Instead of drawing with a crayon or pencil, it is better to use broad tip markers. The larger mark on the paper is easier for the child's vision. It is best to provide a large space for the child to draw. If they are encouraged to draw large pictures, this involves more movement of the shoulder. Ideas for a large writing space include using rolls of blank paper or using a white erase board. Having the child alternate where he draws will incorporate different muscles. For example, drawing on an easel or paper taped to a wall requires standing while drawing and uses more shoulder muscles than sitting at a table. Drawing on paper that is on the floor is good because it requires more postural muscle work. At this age, it continues to be important to provide activities for large shoulder movements. Creativity to use large shoulder muscles can include taking a pail of water and a paint brush or roller and "painting" the sidewalk or block fence.

If a table or desk is to be used, it is important for the feet to touch the ground or to use a built up surface under the feet, such as a phone book. The table top should be about at the level of the child's elbow. It is essential to have the paper as far from his eyes as possible, but allowing the child to have upright posture. Research has shown that from about four to six years of age a child benefits from having his posture supported in this way when doing tasks at a desk. If his posture is not supported, the child pays less attention to the task because he is working to maintain his posture.[82]

These two preschool age girls are demonstrating two ways to draw. When the paper is on the wall the shoulder muscles are more involved. When the paper is on the floor the neck and back muscles are more involved. These are both good foundation building activities!

Television watching is not a recommended foundation building activity and should be kept to an absolute minimum. If a child is watching television, having the child watch television at least six to eight feet away while lying on his tummy will require the child to use some postural muscles and avoid the detrimental visual effects of having the image too close. Another idea for television watching is to provide a large ball that the child must sit on while watching television. This requires the postural muscles to work in contrast to little or no muscle activity used by "couch potatoes".

This girl is watching television while she is sitting on a large ball. Her posture muscles are working hard and she is constantly adjusting her muscles to balance on the ball.

Caution should be used at this age regarding screen time. This includes television, gaming systems and computers. Research is just beginning to look at the changes in the brain as a result of computer use. In 2001, the American Association of Pediatrics recommended that children under the age of two have no screen time and children ages two and over have under two hours per day. In Australia, the recommendation for preschoolers is to have greater than three hours per day spent in physical activity and less than one hour per day for screen time. It is not clear what the total effect is going to be of young children spending increasing time in front of a screen; as of this date, however, there does not appear to be any research showing positive effects. More screen time has been associated with obesity and attention deficit disorders. It is interesting to note that studies show that young children, infants and toddlers who spend much time at a screen become older children who spend much time at a screen. Habits are started early. Parents should use caution!

Even though the preschool years are not the time to emphasize reading or writing, many children in this age group are involved in these activities. Here are some points to consider: Have the material at arm's length away. The pages should not be cluttered with too many visual images and the images must have good visual contrast. Visual contrast would be a bolder print on a light background. It is necessary to stop the activity when signs of fatigue appear. These signs include slouched posture, eyes too close to the material, rubbing eyes and pressing very hard or too light on the writing utensil.

The preschool age continues to be a time that children want to move! They seem to be constantly in motion, and that is a good thing! They are exploring new skills and love to show off! Somersaults are a great skill to work on at this age. (Parents should be sure to assist the child so his chin is on his chest in a tuck position to avoid neck injury). Somersaults reinforce prenatal flexion. This is an age that jumping becomes more developed; children can jump forward and backward and over objects. Hopping is a great skill that develops during these years. Riding a tricycle is a fun and beneficial activity. The importance of playing outside and on playgrounds can not be overemphasized. Taking a child outside to play is a foundation building activity!

Chapter 22

Special Needs Children

All of us have varying degrees of missing information in the building blocks of our foundation. This is easily observed by sitting at an airport and watching the different ways people walk. Some people turn their legs outward, some people hunch forward. Some walk in a bouncing pattern, while others keep their knees slightly bent. The reason for these differences is our sensory-motor foundation. No one has a perfect foundation. Children with special needs are no exception. They also can benefit from having a more solid foundation.

The intent of this chapter is not to recommend particular exercises for specific special needs. It will, however, present how these principles apply to the child with special needs. These examples will be helpful to parents and professionals working in this area. It has been the experience of this therapist that the implementation of these principles helps the progress of many children who have come to a plateau in their skills because of a poor sensory-motor foundation. Children are also less anxious and more focused when these principles are incorporated into their day.

A child who is born prematurely is an example of someone who needs extra work on very early foundational skills. Development of sensory-motor skills begins prenatally; when birth is premature, the time for building these skills is cut short. Being held in the flexed position and listening to the heartbeat in darkness is one way to reinforce some aspects of the sensory environment of the womb and give the child a better foundation for building more advanced motor skills. In addition, since all prenatal touch experiences are wet and slick, activities that use slick, oiled surfaces are helpful in reinforcing those experiences. During the last trimester, a fetus spends time pushing on the uterine wall. Holding a baby in flexion by holding his feet with his legs folded and allowing him to push against resistance can be helpful.

This five-month-old girl with Down syndrome has benefitted from many foundation building activities. She spends much time each day doing tummy time on her plastic mat. When she uses oil, her movements are easy and her hands open more often. Other times in the day she is dressed as in the picture and works hard to get her head up. In the second picture she and her mother are doing hand-tummy rub.

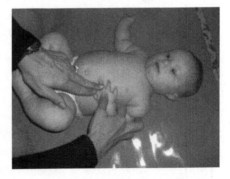

Often children with special needs have muscle tone that is either low or high. An understanding of deep pressure sensation forms one of the building blocks for developing good muscle tone. Doing the deep pressure program outlined in chapter 10 helps "fill" this block and frequently results in improved tone, whether the starting tone is too high or too low. (When used as part of a therapy program, three to five times throughout the day has more of an impact than once a day.). Children, both with and without special needs, who were born by Cesarean section also benefit from a deep pressure program. They have missed the deep pressure experienced in the process of going through the birth canal and benefit from having the "deep pressure" block of their foundation strengthened.

While age-based criteria are helpful in identifying a developmental problem, the ages at which skills should be acquired may be ignored once the problem has been recognized. One should instead focus on those foundational skills which need reinforcing and start there. For example, working on belly crawling helps motor efficiency and visual motor integration. Belly crawling is one of the most important early gross motor skills that contributes to the integration of the nervous system. If the child is already walking, independently or with assistance, go back and check earlier motor skills, such as rolling, creeping and belly crawling—regardless of how old the child is. (Review developmental timeline in Chapter 1.) If the foundation is not firm, walking requires more effort and the child has more difficulty focusing on other tasks, causing stress and fatigue.

> Victor, an older child being seen in therapy, was walking, but had low endurance. He would not even attempt to run a mile in physical education. After extensive work in therapy on foundational skills, including belly crawling, he not only gained the confidence to attempt running a mile, but completed it in less that 12 minutes! Running was never worked on in therapy, but emerged naturally as his foundation became sturdier.

Focusing on building the foundation instead of pushing to higher skills takes longer, but the wait is worth it. Parents and therapists must resist the temptation to take short cuts. While a skill may be learned more quickly, short cuts compromise quality and often increase stress levels. If a child continues to struggle learning a new skill, review the foundational blocks and work to reinforce them. When there is a problem with a skill, the problem is never with the skill. *The problem is in the background*. Often, as soon as a child completes a skill once, it is checked off the list of goals and a new objective becomes the focus. If a skill has a good foundation, it can be repeated without fatigue. A way to avoid pushing skills before a child is ready is to balance a child's activities between new skills and previous sensory-motor skills.

Over the years, both this author and a colleague in occupational therapy have discovered that when they are working with children with cortical visual impairments, there is a correlation between when those children begin belly crawling and a significant improvement in their vision. This is an example of foundation building. By improving the sensory-motor foundation necessary for belly crawling, the higher level function of vision is enhanced.

> Ashley, a child who was struggling academically, had difficulty getting therapy services because she scored so well on evaluation tools. She could do most of the tasks listed for her age level. However, if you asked her to repeat the activity more than one or two times, she would start to fail at the task or simply stare into space. The blocks of her foundation were so shaky that even though she could do many skills, she fatigued too quickly for them to be useful to her in an academic setting. Working on strengthening her foundation did much for improving her school performance.

In general, sensory and gross motor blocks are filled in most easily if there are as few distractions as possible. Bright lights and noises demand the attention of higher levels in the nervous system. Even too many verbal instructions pull the system's attention away from those basic foundational blocks to higher levels. As stated earlier, if a child is struggling in understanding a certain sensation, such as skin sensation necessary for moving an extremity, it may be helpful to diminish other sensations such as lights and noise to see if it is easier for that child to move. Of course, real life isn't in a controlled environment. This suggestion is to pay attention to the sensory environment when a new skill is being learned, not once it has been mastered. This has proven to be invaluable in working with special needs children.

If a child has special needs, these recommendations, as well as the other activities in this book, should be implemented under the direction of the child's therapist. Striving to have a more solid foundation not only makes the child more efficient in using his body but also improves his future capabilities.

Chapter 23

Adoption and Bonding Issues

My husband, Gary, and I have had the privilege of building our family through both birth and adoption. As I have studied the developmental concepts contained in this book and applied them to our family, I have found them to be invaluable with all of our children, but particularly with our sons, who are adopted.

When a child enters a family either by birth or adoption, there are both psychological/emotional and physical facets of the bonding process. Some of these physical aspects include skin-to-skin contact, time spent with the parents and baby simply looking at each other, and the parents becoming familiar with the baby's comforts, such as feeding and warmth. This book contains many activities to enhance the physical aspects of bonding, which leads to a stronger emotional bond. These activities help promote bonding whether the parent-child relationship was developed through birth or adoption.

By utilizing the developmental concepts outlined in this book, the bonding process between the baby and adoptive parents is positively impacted. An occupational therapist, who is a friend and who has also studied these same concepts, shared the following illustration from her experience.

> A woman came to her for help because she felt overwhelmed by the difficulties that her eight-week-old adopted son, Timmy, was having. Timmy did not like to be held, was irritable, and was having difficulty feeding.

All of the mother's attempts to comfort him had failed, and doctors were unable to find anything physically wrong with him. My friend made one primary recommendation. She told Timmy's mother to do deep pressure massage after every diaper change. The woman followed this recommendation. When she returned six weeks later, she reported positive changes. Timmy was eating well and his irritability had greatly decreased; the most remarkable changes had occurred in their relationship. He snuggled in her arms and gazed into her eyes. There was no doubt that he now saw her as his source of security and comfort. Even considering that the baby was now older, he and his mother had more time together, and he had gotten past the "colic" stage, the change was still dramatic. Research has supported the powerful impact of human touch. The deep pressure massage helped Timmy and his mother to connect in a way that was critical to their relationship.

In chapter eight, the need to use "containers" less and to carry baby to promote skin-to-skin contact was discussed. The negative impact of container use, such as carrying a baby in an infant carrier or placing a baby in an ExerSaucer® or swing for prolonged periods of time, is most likely even greater in a child who is adopted. Skin-to-skin contact is critical to the bonding process.

Another important part of the physical environment that will help in bonding is the baby's sense of smell. It is important for the baby to get to know his parent's scent. The sense of smell is a powerful and basic sensation that can be used to assist in bonding.

Our daughter, Alicia, is our biological child. One of the aspects of bonding that I remember most from her birth was the fact that she smelled like me! I was grateful that I knew not to mask that smell during her early infancy to allow her to relate to something familiar. I refrained from using cologne or scented products.

Reinforce previous sensory-motor experiences.

During the time of our sons' entries into our family through adoption, my husband and I were aware of the developmental concepts in this book. Bonding was a different journey with each of our children. Our first son, Blake, was very sensitive to changes in his environment. The bathtub activity and spending time holding him in a dimly blue-lighted room was invaluable. The blue light was a calming activity. He demanded much of our time both day and night for holding him and giving him a sense of security. He received much time with skin-to-skin contact. He was only four months old, but he was aware that everything in his life had changed! Being born in Korea, he now had adults who looked very different, new smells, new formula, and a crib for the first time. By using Key #1, we were able to calm him and allow for his adjustment. These previous sensory-motor experiences included listening to the heartbeat, being in warm water and being curled in flexion; he really calmed when we took him to Asian restaurants! It was comforting for us to know that all of the time he demanded from us when he was a baby was being used to build a strong bond and a strong sensory-motor foundation. Blake is now 24 years old and a successful, secure adult.

Allow baby to grow into higher skills.

Our second son, Tyler, was a year old when he arrived home. We say he landed with both feet in America and has taken charge ever since! Because he was older and more independent, the developmental concepts we used to enhance bonding were a bit different. Deep pressure massage was our most valuable tool. This skin-to-skin contact allowed for a meaningful connection to Tyler and calmed him long enough for him to then enjoy being held in flexion. Even though Tyler was older, we used the baby sling to keep him close to us. He enjoyed sitting in the sling and being with us as we cooked dinner. Key #3 was an important key for the bonding process. The first few months we were especially careful not to push higher skills. We kept Tyler on a bottle and were sure to sit and hold him during feeding times with the bottle. We set up an environment for crawling and playing with big toys to reinforce previous sensor-motor experiences rather than activities that encouraged walking behind toys. (He was close to walking independently when he arrived.) Tyler is now 21 years old and not only is he well adjusted, but has become a definite leader.

The following is a review of some of the recommended developmental activities that especially enhance the parent-infant bond.

Curled in a Flexed Position

Being curled in the flexed position and hearing a heartbeat is extremely comforting to a child. Even toddlers benefit from time spent in a darkened environment, snuggled in their parent's arms and taking a short rest, while listening to the heartbeat sound. This activity provides skin-to-skin contact, warmth, and comfort that enhance the parent-child relationship. The heartbeat sound is provided naturally by placing the child's ear on the parent's chest or by using the heartbeat recording described in Chapter 5. Though some toddlers initially resist this close contact, through repeated, gentle holding, most children come to enjoy it.

Carrying your Baby

When carrying a baby in a plastic carrier, nothing positive is happening to promote bonding. To enhance bonding, a baby should be carried in his parent's arms or in a sling whenever possible. In this way, a baby will be close to his parent's body for security and warmth. This strengthens the connection that a baby makes between his parent and being warm and secure.

Body Smell

A parent's body smell is important in bonding. When a baby is carried in a sling, he has the opportunity to get used to his parent's body smell. It is best that a baby or even an older adopted child learns his parent's smell. Olfaction (the sense of smell) is one of the strongest and most primitive sensory functions in our body. By exposing a baby to a parent's smell, the information system that baby accesses to recognize his parent as a source of security and comfort is strengthened. Perfumes and other fragrances should not be used by the parent during the child's first few months of bonding. Another reason to stay fragrance free is to avoid allergy reactions. Many children and adults have a negative reaction to fragrance. A baby or young child cannot verbalize that reaction, so it is best to eliminate the possibility.

Visual Stimulation

Be sure that there are times when the parent is the primary visual stimulation for the baby. Babies naturally establish "eye contact" with their mothers very quickly. Time spent in a quiet place just having baby and parent looking at each other, singing a song, or doing a lotion rub is valuable. If there is a great deal of visual clutter in a baby's environment, that vital visual connection between a baby and parent may not be established. There is no timetable here. This is all about a relationship. It should be an enjoyable time for both child and parent.

Feeding

Feeding time provides special opportunities for bonding. This is a time when an infant stares at his parent while receiving skin-to-skin contact, warmth, and security. The receptors (sensory nerve endings) that are being stimulated in the mouth contribute to the bonding process as they are often a source of comfort.

Proper positioning during feeding will enhance bonding. During bottle feeding, a baby should be cradled in his parent's arm, with his body held securely next to his parent's body and his parent directly in his line of vision. It is important to give equal time to each side when a child is held for bottle feeding.

With an adopted child who is still on the bottle, this is a time to focus only on the child. Skin-to-skin contact is increased by having a baby touch his parent's face or by having the parent give baby a gentle rub on his arms and legs during feeding.

If the adopted child is a bit older and is still on the bottle, some experts recommend that you get him off the bottle. This author's experience shows that it is best to allow a child to spend a few more months on the bottle, providing the parent is always part of the bottle-feeding process. He will be drinking from a cup for the rest of his life. The bottle is so helpful with bonding. Even if this child can hold his own bottle, he needs to be held and cuddled for several weeks while taking his bottle so that the parent is established as part of the feeding process. The rewards are great for extra time spent on this activity.

If a child is an older toddler when he is adopted and he is not on the bottle, the parent can still use this developmental concept to help with bonding. During some snuggly, quiet times, his face and lips can be gently rubbed. Counting teeth with the parent touching each tooth with his finger allows some sensory nerve endings to be stimulated while intimate parent-child contact is made

Some babies cannot handle the intimacy of the feeding process described above. They prefer to take their bottles while facing away from the parents and would rather be held loosely than snuggled. Initially, parents must do whatever works to make feeding a success.

Understand that this baby is having some problems bonding or with the over-all sensory experience. This child needs gentle work on a more intimate feeding session. Learning to read a baby's signs of distress and not crossing into the areas that provoke distress is critical. Parents should introduce this baby each day to more snuggling and eye contact so that bonding increases.

Bathtub Activity

An infant will develop a sense of trust primarily through his skin sensations. The bathtub activity described in Chapter 9 has proven to be helpful in building this trust and, therefore, promotes the bonding process. This activity of warm water, dim lighting, and much skin-to-skin contact enhances relaxation while contributing to the parent-infant relationship. See Chapter 9 for more details.

Deep Pressure Massage

Deep pressure massage is wonderful for bonding. The skin and muscle receptors are stimulated, with a resulting "sense of well being." This is an excellent relationship builder. Deep pressure massage is described in Chapter 10.

Illness or Pain

As difficult as times are when a baby becomes sick or gets a painful ear infection, they are perfect opportunities for bonding. When the parent is the source of comfort and pain relief, bonds are formed. Whenever possible, have it be the parent who takes the time to be there for baby during these difficult times. The first months of having a child join a family through adoption are not the time to worry about spoiling the baby.

Go Slowly, If Necessary

Most babies who are adopted accept these activities well from the first time they are started. However, there are other babies who do not. Be sensitive to their tolerance. As I mentioned previously, some young babies cannot initially handle eye contact during feeding time. It demands too much from them, both physically and emotionally. Some babies would rather be in a plastic seat than being held. They are truly happiest when no one is interacting with them. These babies should not be forced to interact, but keep in mind that this is not a good place to leave the relationship. Starting slowly is important. Doing the oil activities on a piece of vinyl or plastic may be a good place to start. The baby is on his tummy while the parent is massaging him. In this way, he does not have to deal with being held or making eye contact. After a few days of this activity, he may be ready for more holding and then may progress to making more eye contact. Getting to know a baby and what he likes helps guide this process. Gently adding good developmental activities until his comfort zone expands fills in the blocks of his sensory-motor foundation.

What if all is not going well?

Just because bonding is not going well, parents must not assume there will be future problems. It is also important not to assume that because a baby does not like to be held or does not like massage, he will always be like this. Sensory-motor systems are very pliable. They build upon experience. If there is concern about problems in bonding and these suggestions do not help, parents should contact a professional for more specific recommendations. The adoption agency and the pediatrician are excellent resources for help. There is always room for hope in the area of bonding. It may require a bit more work or time, but the rewards and joy are immeasurable and last a lifetime!

Conclusion

In a world that is getting more complex each day, it is reassuring to know that we can have a positive impact on our children using six basic key principles. By presenting these key principles, my hope is that parents will begin to integrate this knowledge into the decisions they are making for their child. More importantly, I hope that parents will gain a better understanding of their child. The better the child's development and individual strengths are understood, the better able the parent is to make informed decisions for their child.

Writing this book was a labor of love for me, but it was not easy. My book is the effort of many years of experience and study, but most importantly it is the effort of many people sharing their experiences. To be honest, there have been times when I have wondered whether all the time and effort has been worth it. It seems that every time I have these thoughts, I have an encounter with someone who shares with me the impact this book has made for them. This happened yesterday as I was struggling on how to conclude this book. A mother of two children, ages 2 and 3, shared with me how having read *Building Babies Better* before the adoption of her first child and then again after the birth of her second child continues to impact her family. Among the things she shared were how she has learned to observe how various activities impact her child's postural system. She has limited "screen time" because of these observations and has even concluded that something positive, like reading books, when done for too long of a time period can have a negative impact on her children's sensory-motor system. She tries hard to do all activities in balance, including changing postures when the children play with paper and pencil. She is even using some of the key principles from *Building Babies Better* to determine when her children will be ready for preschool. The best statement she shared with me is that she feels these key principles took a lot of stress off of her and she feels much more confident in her parenting! This young mother summed up the goals and potential impacts of this book. She certainly lifted my spirits!

I urge you that now is the time to focus on building a solid foundation for your child. We must withstand our culture's constant prodding to buy more toys, enroll our babies in more classes, and get them walking, talking and reading as early as possible. I have seen that this frantic pace creates unnecessary stress for both children and parents. The world provides enough stress on its own, as we are all aware. Instead, I encourage you to relax and enjoy your child. I want you to be confident that more is not always better and to rid yourself of the guilt caused by not doing enough to stimulate your baby's development.

It is my hope that we can begin to change regular environments into developmental environments that will build solid sensory-motor foundations. My goal in writing *Building Babies Better* is to provide the tools necessary to help a child develop into a sturdy adult—one who can hold up to life's stresses and not only survive, but thrive! Focusing on this long-term goal is what *Building Babies Better* is all about.

Enjoy building!

Notes

These references and notes are provided to encourage the reader to dig deeper into the literature for a more complete understanding of developmental issues. The author has provided comments and/or quotes from the cited material that were meaningful to the author.

Introduction

1. Hadders-Algra M (2000). The Neuronal Group Selection Theory: a framework to explain variation in normal motor development. *Dev Med & Child Neurol.*42:566-572
    ("According to the NGST, variation is the keyword for normal development." This implies that having a variety of options for movement is a critical part of normal development.)

2. Pin T, Eldridge B, Galea M (2007). A review of the effects of sleep position, play position, and equipment use on motor development in infants. *Dev Med & Child Neurol.* 49:858-867
    (These authors reviewed the literature and found that few studies look at the quality of movement but rather look at milestone checklists. "Like the sleep/play positions, it is unclear whether there were any subtle differences in the movement quality of equipment users later in their childhood. There is limited research on other infant equipment such as different infant seats, car seats, and swings, which have become increasingly more popular in use than the baby walker in recent times.")

Chapter 1

Sensory-Motor Development

3. Adolph KE, Vereijken B, Denny MA. (1998). Learning to crawl. *Child Development* 69:1299-312
    (Crawling proficiency is better in infants who previously were belly crawlers than in infants who skipped the stage of belly crawling.)

4. Alexander R, Boehme R, Cupps B (1993). *The First Year of Life*; Tucson, Az; Therapy Skill Builders Publishing
    (This includes a review of the sequence of gross motor development.)

5. Campbell S, Vander Linden D, Palisano R (Ed) (2006). *Physical Therapy for Children 3rd Edition;* St Louis, Missouri; Saunders Elsevier Publishing
    (Pg 37 discussing Dynamical Systems Theory . . . "In this model of infant motor development, therefore, the environment is as important as the organism.")

6. Dudek-Shriber L, Zelazny S (2007). The effects of prone positioning on the Quality and Acquisition of Developmental Milestones in Four-month Old Infants. *Pediatric Phys Ther.* Spring: 19(1)48-55
    ("Time spent in the prone position while awake however was found to be significant to the four-month-old infant's achievement of seven of the 21 prone, three of the nine supine, and three of the 12 sitting milestones.")

7. Hadders-Algra M (2000). The Neuronal Group Selection Theory: a framework to explain variation in normal motor development. *Dev Med & Child Neurol.*42:566-572
    ("According to the NGST, variation is the keyword for normal development. The variation is not random, but

determined by criteria set by genetic information." "The theory highlights the notion that development is the result of a complex intertwining of information from genes and environment.")

8. Jeng, SF, Chen LC, Tsou, KI, Chen W, Lou, H (2004) Relationship Between Spontaneous Kicking and Age of Walking Attainment in Preterm Infants With Very Low Birth Weight and Full Term Infants; *Phys Ther*;84:159-172 (This study established mean age of normal attainment of walking at 12 months with range at 9-15 months.)

9. Littlefield T, Kelly K, Reiff J, Pomatto J (2003). Car Seats, Infant Carriers, and Swings: Their Role in Deformational Plagiocephaly. *J Prosthetics and Orthotics*; July 15 (3): 102-106 (Not only did the "Back to Sleep" Campaign increase the incidence of deformational plagiocephaly but extended time spent by infants in positioning devices [containers] also contributes to this deformity. Deformities caused by extended time spent in "containers" show a distinctive and often times more severe deformity.)

10. Majnemer A, Barr RG (2005). Influence of supine sleep positioning on early motor milestone acquisition. *Dev Med Child Neurol.* Jan;47(6):370-376 (Infant motor development involves an intricate interplay between maturity of the musculoskeletal and nervous system and extrinsic experiences. Maturational readiness and daily opportunities for practice enable infants to achieve developmental milestones.)

11. Miller L, Johnson A, Duggan L, Behm M (2011). Consequences of the "Back to Sleep" Program in Infants. *Journal of Pediatric Nursing* 26:364-368

(Since the initial recommendation by the AAP [American Academy of Pediatrics], there has been a 44% decline in the SIDS rate from 1.20 per 1,000 live births to 0.67.)

12. Slater A, Lewis M ed (2006). *Introduction to Infant Development* Oxford University Press. New York Pgs 42-63 (Hepper, P)
(This author discusses prenatal development and how this acts as a foundation on which all subsequent development builds. ". . . these abilities [abilities of the newborn] have their origins in the prenatal period, implying a continuity of development across the birth period.")

13. Thelen E, Spencer JP (1998). Postural control during reaching in young infants: a dynamic systems approach. *Neurosci Biobehav Rev*. Jul:22(4):507-14
("Motor development proceeds as a continual dialogue between the nervous system, body, and environment.")

14. Wallace M, Carriere B, Perrault T, Vaughan J, Stein B (2006). The Development of Cortical Multisensory Integration. *Journal of Neuroscience*. Nov:26(46):11844-11849
("The present results reveal a sequential and sensory-specific maturation of AES during postnatal life." This study was done on cats looking at the AES [anterior ectosylvian sulcus], which is a cortical structure in the cat responsible for multisensory integration. The conclusions suggest that multisensory integrative capacity matures gradually in postnatal development and has a specific order.)

Chapter 2

Keys for Good Sensory-Motor Development

Key #1 Reinforce previous sensory-motor experiences.

15. Bekhoff A, Kauer JA. (1984). Neural control of hatching: fate of the pattern generator for the leg movements of hatching in post hatching chicks. *J. Neurosci.* 4(11): 2659-2666
(This is a study done on chicks. They found that a specific leg movement pattern only seen in this animal during the hatching process could be produced in older chicks when they were gently folded into the hatching position and placed in artificial eggs. This supports the concept that changing the environment to a previous developmental environment can result in the emergence of a previous movement pattern associated with that environment.)

Key #2 Gross motor comes before fine motor.

16. Iverson, J.M. (2010). Developing language in a developing body: The relationship between motor development and language development. *Journal of Child Language,* 37,339-261.
("Motor acquisitions provide infants with an opportunity to practice skills relevant to language acquisition before they are needed for that purpose. Emergence of new motor skills changes infants experience with objects and people in ways that are relevant for both general communicative development and the acquisition of language.")

17. Reilly D, van Donkelaar P, Saavedra S, Woollacott M (2008). Interaction Between the Development of Postural Control and the Executive Function of Attention. *J Mot Behav*; March 40(2):90-102

("The younger children, with less maturation of the two systems, (postural control and development of executive attention) experienced postural control interference that increased when the attentional load of the postural task increased. Therefore, early childhood educators should consider that interaction when planning an academic curriculum and creating an environment most conducive to learning. In younger children, an attentionally demanding cognitive task may overload the naturally limited attentional resources, resulting in postural control interference and manifesting as extraneous movements.")

18. Saavedra S, Woollacott M, van Donkelaar P. (2007) Effects of postural support on eye hand interactions across development: *Exp Brain Res* 180:557-567
("Trunk postural control is a necessary requirement for the development of accurate reaching skills.")

19. Thelen E, Spencer JP (1998) Postural control during reaching in young infants: a dynamic systems approach. *Neurosci Biobehav Rev*. Jul:22(4):507-14
("The goal of postural stability must be maintained during a reach. Motor development proceeds as a continual dialogue between the nervous system, body, and environment.")

Key #3 Allow baby to grow into higher skills.

20. Turkewitz G, Kenny PA (1982) The Role of Developmental Limitations of Sensory Input on Sensory / Perceptual Organization *Dev Psychobiol*. Jul 15 (4):357-68
(Limited sensory capacities that are normal in the early stages of life provide an organizational framework for development. The timing of functional onset of the various systems in relation to one another is of great importance.)

21. Uchiyama I, Anderson D, Campos J, Witherington, D, Frankel C, Lejeune L, Barbu-Roth, M (2008) Locomotor Experience Affects Self and Emotion; *Dev Psych*; Vol 44 (5); 1225-1231

(These authors cited studies dealing with the influence of locomotion [both self-locomotion as well as artificial locomotion as in the use of a baby walker] on both postural compensation as well as the emotional reaction to peripheral optic flow. The peripheral optic flow was caused by a moving room apparatus. Their conclusions included that locomotor infants, whether crawling or in a walker, respond more adaptively to the peripheral optic flow than non-locomotor infants. The point being that placing a baby in a walker for early locomotion has an impact on other developmental systems. The authors state, "If locomotor experience is provided at too early an age, the other skills required to effect a developmental reorganization may not yet be in place.")

22. Wallace M, Stein B (2007). Early Experience Determines How the Senses Will Interact. *J Neurophysiol*. 97: 921-926

("The earliest appearing multisensory neurons in the superior colliculus [SC] are incapable of synthesizing cross-modal stimuli. Rather, they require a protracted period of postnatal maturation to develop this capability, suggesting that sensory experience could be an important determinant." "Presumably, multisensory maturation is protracted because considerable time is needed to gather the experience with combinations of cross-modal cues necessary to link them to common environmental events and to each other.")

Key #4 Encourage activities that use both sides of the body.

23.   Goldfield EC, Michel GF(1986). Spatiotemporal linkage in Infant interlimb Coordination. *Dev Psychobiol*. 19(3):259-64

(In a study of seven-month and 11-month-old infants looking at interlimb coordination of reaching, it was found that by three months of age infants begin to extend both hands to the midline to touch an object, at seven months of age simultaneity of hand movement was still prevalent, but by 11 months of age movement of hands was primarily done in complementary movements rather than simultaneous movements.)

24. Sparling JW, Van Tol J, Chescheir NC (1999). Fetal and Neonatal Hand Movement. *Phys Ther*; 79:24-39
(The author's chart shows at 20 weeks gestation there is more bilateral movement, for example, legs extend together against uterine wall, arms flex, hands held together near face. At 26 to 32 weeks gestation there is more independent movement of extremities to all parts of the uterus and specific body parts.)

Key #5 Avoid small, detailed visual images.

25. Christakis DA, Zimmerman FJ, DiGiuseppe DL, McCarty CA (2004). Early television exposure and subsequent attentional problems in children. *Pediatrics*; Apr: 113(4) 708-13
(Results from a study of 1278 children at age 1 and 1345 children at age 3 showed the hours of television viewed per day at both ages 1 and 3 was associated with attentional problems at age 7. The more hours of TV was correlated with an increase of attention problems.)

26. Dai S (2010) Visual impairment in children from myopia: can it be prevented? *Clin Experiment Ophthalmol.* Apr (3):229-30
(Current knowledge of the relationship between the intensity of near work and progression of myopia and the protective factor of outdoor activities in the development of myopia

has significant clinical implications for tackling the growing problem of myopia. The promotion of healthy vision habits among school children, such as limiting the hours per day spent on books and computer work, and increasing outdoor activities, may well help us to prevent the onset and progression of myopia.)

27. Doidge, N (2007). *The Brain that changes itself.* Penguin Group Publishing. New York Pgs 210-212
(In discussing work by Pascual-Leone this author states, "Absolute darkness was essential to the change [for visual cortices to process the sense of touch] because vision is so powerful a sense that if any light got in, the visual cortex preferred to process it over sound and touch." . . . "our brains are not truly organized in terms of systems that process a given sensory modality. Rather, our brain is organized in a series of specific operators." "An operator is selected by competition.")

28. Eliot, L (2000). *What's Going On in There? How the Brain and Mind Develop in the First Five Years of Life.* Bantam Publishing. New York.
Chapter 9 pgs 196-227
(Less visual acuity in the first 6 months of life helps protect from over stimulation. It is not until around 12 months of age that vision is almost like an adult's. It isn't until between 3 and 6 months of age that a baby can choose where to look. This obligatory looking prior to this age stimulates the cortex and can cause distress. The fovea of the eye's retina is used for all fine vision and it is the slowest part of the retina to mature.)

29. Kenny PA, Turkewitz G (1986). Effects of unusually early visual stimulation on the development of homing behavior in the rat pup *Dev Psychobiol* Jan; 19(1):57-66

(An animal study that showed premature eyelid opening resulted in a modification of both visual and olfactory attention. Premature use of one sensory system developmentally had an impact on other sensory systems.)

30. Slater A, Lewis M ed (2006). *Introduction to Infant Development* Oxford University Press. New York Pgs 42-63 (Hepper, P)
(In a discussion by the author regarding newborn senses, he states, "However of all the senses, the visual sense is least well developed.")

Key #6 Play within limits of fatigue.

31. SC Gandevia (2001). Spinal and Supraspinal Factors in Human Muscle Fatigue
Physiol Rev 81:1725-1789
(Peripheral fatigue includes muscle fatigue. Central fatigue [first noted in 1996] is supraspinal fatigue and includes the cortex. This supports the concept of neurological fatigue.)

Part I

Early Infancy
Birth through Six Months

Chapter 3

Feeding Considerations

32. Lawrence R (1995). The clinician's role in teaching proper infant feeding techniques. *JPediatr.* 126(6):S112-7.
(The process of breast feeding is as beneficial as the nutrition. When bottle feeding, it is best to imitate nursing. By having the baby semi-reclined it eliminates the entry of milk into the middle ear. It also reduces choking and spitting up. Direct eye contact helps bonding and the close body contact promotes a sense of security in the child.)

Chapter 4

Visual Environment

33. Brunborg GS, Mentzoni RZ, Molde H, Myrseth H, Skouveroe KJ, Bjorvatn B, Pallesen S (2011). The relationship between media use in the bedroom, sleep habits and symptoms of insomnia. *J Sleep Res.* Feb 16
(This study indicates that the use of computers and mobile telephones in the bedroom are related to poor sleep habits.)

34. Doidge, N (2007). *The Brain that changes itself.* Penguin Group Publishing. New York Pgs 210-212
(In discussing work by Pascual-Leone this author states, "Absolute darkness was essential to the change [for visual cortices to process touch] because vision is so powerful a

sense that if any light got in, the visual cortex preferred to process it over sound and touch.")

35. Harrison EM, Gorman MR, Mednich SC (2011)The effect of narrowband 500 nm light on daytime sleep in humans. *Physiol Behav*. May 3; 103(2); 197-202
("Although light has various alerting effects at night, 500 nm LED light presented via light mask does not appear to inhibit daytime sleep.)

36. Hussey-Gardner, B (2008). *Understanding My Signals: Help for Parents of Premature Infants*. Vort Corp Publishing. Palo Alto
(This publication shows premature babies giving signals when they may be unhappy. These include the "salute" of eye covering, spreading fingers apart, frown, or grimace. Sometimes arching, yawning and looking away signal unhappiness.)

37. Martuzzi R, Murray MM, Michel Lm, Thiran, JP, Maeder PP, Clake S, Meuli RR (2007). Multi-sensory interactions within human primary cortices revealed by BOLD dynamics. *Cereb Cortex*.17(7): 1672-9.
("Simple noise burst activated primary visual cortices and simple visual stimuli, checkerboards, activated primary auditory cortices." This is indicative of multisensory convergence. This information speaks to the importance of having times when baby's environment is less complicated in regards to sensory input. These less complicated times could be darkness or quiet, allowing less interference from competing sensory inputs while building the sensory-motor foundation.)

38. Miller L, Johnson A, Duggan L, Behm M (2011). Consequences of the "Back to Sleep" Program in Infants. *Journal of Pediatric Nursing* 26:364-368

(Suggestions to avoid unnecessary consequences of the "Back to Sleep" campaign include limiting time the infant is on their back in car seats, infant swings, and infant carriers. Another suggestion is to reverse the head-to-toe position of the infant's crib weekly.)

Chapter 5

Auditory Environment during Early Infancy

39. Barnard KE, Bee HL (1983). The Impact of temporally patterned stimulation on the development of preterm infants. *Child Dev* 54 (5):1156-7
(Heartbeat sounds introduced into the incubators of preterm babies improved their mental development as measured at 2 years of age.)

40. Eliot, L (2000). *What's Going On in There? How the Brain and Mind Develop in the First Five Years of Life.* Bantam Publishing. New York
Chapter 10 pgs 228-259
(The development of hearing beginning prenatally is described. A fetus can hear mother's heartbeat and blood flow, which provide a constant, low-frequency back beat.)

Chapter 6

Tummy Time Activity

41. Chizawsky LL, Scott-Findlay S (2005). Tummy time: Preventing unwanted effects of the "Back to Sleep" campaign. *AWHONN Lifelines.* Oct-Nov9(5):382-387
(Physicians and therapists commonly use motor milestones to evaluate normal developmental progress in infants and

children. Research is now showing that the change in sleep position has slowed the attainment of gross motor skills, including rolling over, sitting up, crawling, and pulling to a standing position by reducing opportunities for practice of these skills, which are best developed in the prone position.)

42. Dudek-Shriber L, Zelazny S (2007). The effects of prone positioning on the Quality and Acquisition of Developmental Milestones in Four-month Old Infants. *Pediatric Phys Ther.* Spring: 19(1)48-55

("Time spent in the prone position while awake however was found to be significant to the four-month old infant's achievement of seven of the 21 prone, three of the nine supine, and three of the 12 sitting milestones." "The results of this study also appear to suggest that those infants who spent slightly more than an hour or more in the prone position while awake per day achieved greater success in acquiring certain prone, supine, and sitting milestones that begin developing incrementally at approximately four months of age.")

43. Jennings JT, Sarbaugh BG, Payne NS (2005). Conveying the message about optimal infant positions. *Phys Occup Ther Pediatr*; 25(3):3-18

(The average Peabody Developmental Motor Scales-2 locomotion score of the babies regularly placed in prone was significantly higher than that of the babies not regularly placed in prone when tested at 6 months and again at 18 months of age.)

44. Majnemer A, Barr RG (2006) Association between sleep position and early motor development. *Jpediatr.* Nov: 149(5):623-629

("It is increasingly appreciated that environmental characteristics such as care giving practices can influence the timing of acquisition of early motor milestones." "We provide empirical evidence demonstrating that exposure to awake prone position is positively correlated with motor scores [PDMS and AIMS] at 4 months and especially at 6 months.")

45. Miller L, Johnson A, Duggan L, Behm M (2011). Consequences of the "Back to Sleep" Program in Infants. *Journal of Pediatric Nursing* 26:364-368
("The primary intervention to decrease the risk of plagiocephaly is "tummy time.")

46. Monson RM, Deitz J, Kartin D (2003). The relationship between awake positioning and motor performance among infants who slept supine. *Pediatr Phys Ther.* Winter; 15 (4): 196-203
("Gross motor performance as measured by the AIMS was more advanced in infants who slept supine and had been placed in the prone position when awake than in infants who slept supine but had limited or no experience in the prone position while awake.")

47. Rocha NA, Tudella E (2008). The influence of lying positions and postural control on hand-mouth and hand-hand behaviors in 0-4 month old infants. *Infant Behav Dev.* Jan;31(1):107-14
(Babies under the age of four months put hands in mouth when on stomach or side lying much more often and for longer periods than when lying on their back.)

Chapter 7

Tummy-Leg Rub Activity

48. Field T (1995). Massage therapy for infants and children. *J Dev Behav Pediatr;* 16:105-111

(This study was done on infants and children with various medical conditions. Massage therapy resulted in lower anxiety and stress hormones and improved clinical courses.)

49. Kulkarni A, Kaushik JS, Gupta P, Sharma H, Agrawal RK (2010). Massage and touch therapy in neonates: the current evidence. *Indian Pediatr*; 47(9):771-6
("Massage has several positive effects in terms of weight gain, better sleep-wake pattern, enhanced neuromotor development, better emotional bonding, reduced rates of nosocomial infection [hospital acquired infection] and thereby, reduced mortality in the hospitalized patients." "Massage was found to be more useful when some kind of lubricant oil was used.")

50. Montagu A (1986). *Touching: The Human Significance of the Skin*, 3rd Ed. N. Y. Harper and Row Publishers.
("Among the most important of the newborn infant's needs are the signals it receives through the skin, its first medium of communication with the outside world." [Pg 57] "The early development of the nervous system of the infant is to a major extent dependent upon the kind of cutaneous stimulation it receives. There can be no doubt that tactile stimulation is necessary for its healthy development." [Pg 241])

Chapter 8

Carrying Baby

51. Abbott AL, Bartlett DJ (2001) Infant motor development and equipment use in the home. *Child Care Health Dev*; May;27(3): 295-306
(Forty three mothers and their eight-month-old infants were recruited in this study done in Canada. Equipment use was determined by parental survey and infant motor development

was assessed using the AIMS. The findings suggested that infants who have high equipment use tend to score lower on infant motor development and that infants who have low equipment use tend to score higher on infant motor development.)

52. Feldman R, Eidelman Al, Sirota L, Weller A (2002). Comparison of skin-to-skin (Kangaroo) and Traditional Care: Parenting Outcomes and Preterm Infant Development. *Pediatr*; 110:16-26
(Kangaroo care is parent-infant skin-to-skin contact. "Kangaroo care had a significant positive impact on the infant's perceptual-cognitive and motor development and on the parenting process. We speculate that KC has both a direct impact on infant development by contributing to neurophysiologic organization and an indirect effect by improving parental mood, perceptions, and interactive behavior.")

53. Hill S, Engle S, Jorgensen J, Dralik A, Whitman K (2005). Effects of facilitated tucking during routine care of infants born preterm. *Pediatr Phys Ther*; Summer 17(2)158-163
(A study of 12 infants born preterm showed that facilitated tucking [caregiver held the infants in the flexed position] during routine care events reduced the stress level in 9 of the 12 infants.)

54. Littlefield T, Kelly K, Reiff J, Pomatto J (2003). Car Seats, Infant Carriers, and Swings: Their Role in Deformational Plagiocephaly. *J Prosthetics and Orthotics*; July 15 (3): 102-106
(Not only did the "Back to Sleep" Campaign increase the incidence of deformational plagiocephaly but extended time spent by infants in positioning devices [containers] also contributes to this deformity. Deformities caused by

extended time spent in "containers" show a distinctive and often times more severe deformity.)

Chapter 9

Bathtub Activity

55. Feldman R, Eidelman Al, Sirota L, Weller A (2002). Comparison of skin-to-skin (Kangaroo) and Traditional Care: Parenting Outcomes and Preterm Infant Development. *Pediatr*; 110:16-26
(Skin to skin contact between parent and infant has a positive impact on the infant's perceptual-cognitive and motor development and on the parenting process.)

56. Montagu A (1986). *Touching: The Human Significance of the Skin*, 3rd Ed. N. Y. Harper and Row Publishers.
("Sometimes a baby, when put to nurse at the mother's breast, will fail to suckle and appear unable to take the nipple into the mouth. This usually occurs when the baby is wrapped in a towel or some other material. When it is removed and the baby's skin allowed to come into contact with the mother's skin, the baby will usually begin to suckle." Pg 83)

Chapter 10

Massage and Deep Pressure

57. Field T, Diego MA, Hernandez-Reif M, Deeds O, Figuereido B (2006). Moderate versus light pressure massage therapy leads to greater weight gain in preterm infants. *Infant Behav Dev*; Dec; 29(4):574-8

(Using moderate pressure massage leads to a greater weight gain in preterm infants compared to using light pressure massage.)

58. Kulkarni A, Kaushik JS, Gupta P, Sharma H, Agrawal RK (2010). Massage and touch therapy in neonates: the current evidence. *Indian Pediatr*; 47(9):771-6
("Massage has several positive effects in terms of weight gain, better sleep-wake pattern, enhanced neuromotor development, better emotional bonding, reduced rates of nosocomial infection [hospital-acquired infection] and thereby, reduced mortality in the hospitalized patients." "A conducive environment needs to be established before initiation of massage. A room with soft light, warm temperature, and low noise levels is ideal.")

Chapter 11

Activities to Avoid

59. Abbott AL, Bartlett DJ (2001) Infant motor development and equipment use in the home. *Child Care Health Dev*; May;27(3): 295-306
(Forty three mothers and their eight-month-old infants were recruited in this study done in Canada. Equipment use was determined by parental survey and infant motor development was assessed using the AIMS. The findings suggested that infants who have high equipment use tend to score lower on infant motor development and that infants who have low equipment use tend to score higher on infant motor development.)

60. Cavalier A, Picot MC, Artiaga C, Mazurier E, Amilhau MO, Froye, E, Catier G, Picaud JC (2011). Prevention of

deformational plagiocephaly in neonates. *Early Hum Dev*; Aug:87(8): 537-43

(Following a control group and an intervention group during the neonatal months showed that training parents in proper positioning for unhindered movement [less container time] reduced the prevalence of deformational plagiocephaly.)

61. Littlefield T, Kelly K, Reiff J, Pomatto J (2003). Car Seats, Infant Carriers, and Swings: Their Role in Deformational Plagiocephaly. *J Prosthetics and Orthotics*; July 15 (3): 102-106

(Not only did the "Back to Sleep" Campaign increase the incidence of deformational plagiocephaly but extended time spent by infants in positioning devices [containers] also contributes to this deformity. Deformities caused by extended time spent in "containers" shows a distinctive and often times more severe deformity.)

62. Littlefield TR, Saba NM, Kelly KM (2004). On the current incidence of deformational plagiocephaly: an estimation based on prospective registration at a single center. *Seminars in Pediatric Neurology* Dec;11(4): 301-304

(Of the 342 infants, 86% of infants were said to sleep primarily supine or on their side, and 15.2% reported plagiocephaly, a dramatic increase from the 1974 incidence, when only 0.33% of infants presented with plagiocephaly.)

63. Myers CT, Yuen HK, Walker KF (2006). The use of infant seating devices in child care centers. *Am J Occup Ther*. 60(5):489-93

(Infants at 4 months of age in child care centers spend significantly more time in a seating device during the day than they do on the floor or being held.)

64. Siegel AC, Burton RV (1999). Effects of baby walkers on motor and mental development in human infants. *J Dev Behav Pediatr*; 20(5):355-361

("This study analyzed motor and mental development in 109 human infants, with and without walker experience, between the ages of 6 and 15 months. Walker experienced infants sat, crawled, and walked later than no-walker controls, and they scored lower on Bayley scales of mental and motor development.)

65. Uchiyama I, Anderson DI, Campos JJ, Witherington D, Frankel CB, Lejeune L, Barbu-Roth M (2008). Locomotor Experience Affects Self and Emotion. *Dev Psychol*; Sep:44(5):1225-31

(This study supports that the use of a baby walker impacts systems other than just the motor system.)

Part II

Older Baby
Six Months through Beginning to Walk

Chapter 14

Slick Surface for Belly Crawling

66. Adolph KE, VereijkenB, Denny MA. (1998). Learning to crawl. *Child Development* 69:1299-312
(Crawling [hands and knees] proficiency is better in infants who previously were belly crawlers, than in infants who skipped the stage of belly crawling.)

67. Campos JJ, Anderson DI, Barbu-Roth MA, Hubbard EM, Hertenstein MJ, Witherington D. (2000). Travel broadens the mind. *Infancy*, 1, 149-219
("We propose that the origins of these changes [infant's new autonomy] in the infant, the parent, and the family system come from prone progression and not, as they [previous researchers] maintained, principally from upright locomotion.")

68. Thelen E (1985). Developmental origins of motor co-ordination: leg movements in human infants. *Dev Psychobiol*; Jan: 18(1):1-22
(This speaks to the possibility of the importance of belly crawling. Leg movements in early infancy have an inflexible pattern of movement in which the hip, knee, and ankle move as a unit. During the first year of development, the movements become more complex, and the relationship between the different leg segments becomes more dissociated.)

Chapter 15

Sitting

69. deGraaf-Peters VB, Bakker H, van Eykern LA, Otten B, Hadders-Algra M (2007). Postural adjustments and reaching in 4—and 6-month-old infants: an EMG and kinematical study. *Exp Brain Res*; Aug; 181(4):647-56
("Already from 4 months onward a better postural control is associated with a larger success and a better quality of reaching.")

70. Iverson, J.M. (2010). Developing language in a developing body: The relationship between motor development and language development. *Journal of Child Language*, 37,339-261.
(Unsupported independent sitting allows the rib cage to be freed and unsupported independent sitting infants can breathe more deeply and maintain subglottal pressure more consistently than in supine. This effect does not occur if sitting in a container.)

71. Shumway-Cook, A., & Woollacott, M. (2001). *Motor Control: Theory and Practical Applications*. Lippincott, Williams, and Wilkins. Philadelphia, USA.
(pg 206-7 "By 8 months of age, when infants had mastered independent sitting, muscles in the neck and trunk were coordinated into effective patterns for controlling forward and backward sway in the seated position.")

Chapter 16

Fine Motor Skills

72. Saavedra S, Woollacott M, vanDonKelaar P (2007). Effects of postural support on eye hand interactions across development. *Exp Brain Res* 180:557-567 (Improved trunk control is related to improved eye-hand control.)

73. Shumway-Cook, A., & Woollacott, M. (2001). *Motor Control: Theory and Practical Applications.* Lippincott, Williams, and Wilkins. Philadelphia, USA. (pg 476-83). (Visually guided reaching matures at 7 months, whereas precision grasping [objects grasped between index and thumb] does not develop until 9-13 months of age.)

Chapter 18

Play While Creeping on Hands and Knees

74. Campos JJ, Anderson DI, Barbu-Roth MA, Hubbard EM, Hertenstein MJ, Witherington D. (2000). Travel broadens the mind. *Infancy*, 1, 149-219 ("Locomotor experience fine tunes the development of distance perception.")

75. Wannier T, Bastiaanse C, Colombo G, Dietz V (2001). Arm to leg co-ordination in humans during walking, creeping, and swimming activities. *Exp Brain Res*; Dec: 141(3): 375-9 (Characteristics of creeping are tied to walking.)

Chapter 19

Activities to Avoid

76. *American Academy of Pediatrics Policy Statement: Injuries Associated with Infant Walkers.* (2001). Retrieved November 10, 2011 from http://aappolicy.aapublications.org/cgi/content/full/pediatrics;108/3/790
(The AAP recommends a ban on the manufacture and sale of mobile infant walkers.)

77. *Children's Memorial Hospital: Basic gear to foster motor development.* (2009). Retrieved November 10, 2011 from http://www.childrensmemorial.org/depts/rehab/motor-development.aspx
(This is a summary from rehabilitative services at Children's Memorial Hospital in Chicago. It addresses recommended equipment for babies as well as equipment and toys to avoid.)

78. Christakis, DA (2009). The effects of infant media usage: what do we know and what should we learn? *Acta Paediatr*: Jan; 98 (1):8-16
(Television exposure during infancy is associated with language delays and attentional problems. Recommendation was children under the age of two be discouraged from watching television. Even if the TV show is intended for the adults, there can be a negative effect on the child.)

79. Ezzo M (2002). *Your Child's Mind.* Solid Foundations Publishing. Cottage Grove, MN
(This author describes how the brain processes information from the TV. The fast paced visual images and the constant change in auditory volume continually bombard the attention centers of the brain. Pgs 58-64)

Part III

Special Issues

Chapter 21

Beyond the Age of One

80. Barr R (2010). Transfer of learning between 2D and 3D sources during infancy: Informing theory and practice. *Dev Rev*: Jun 1;30(2): 128-154
(The video deficit effect refers to the fact that infants' ability to transfer learning from television and still 2D images to real-life situations is poor relative to their ability to transfer learning from face-to-face interactions. The video deficit effect is non-apparent at 6 months of age, peaks around 15 months of age, and persists until at least 36 months of age depending on the task complexity.)

81. Foudriat BA, DiFabio RP, Anderson JA(1993). Sensory organization of balance responses in children 3-6 years of age: a normative study with diagnostic implications. *Int J Pediatr Otorhinolaryngol*; Oct: 27 (3): 255-71
(This establishes that balance reactions in early development are primarily driven by visual-vestibular systems and at around age 3 they become primarily driven by the somatosensory system. Somatosensory includes skin sensations, muscles sensations and body position. This gives importance to the skin and muscle pressure experiences of the first year of life which will form the foundation for balance reactions around three years of age.)

82. Reilly D, van Donkelaar P, Saavedra S, Woollacott M (2008). Interaction Between the Development of Postural Control

and the Executive Function of Attention. *J Mot Behav*; March 40(2):90-102

(When young children, ages 4-6, are given a task of executive function of attention, they sustain the greatest dual-task interference [as compared to older age groups], evident in decrease in postural control. Their performance of an intentionally demanding cognitive task would be enhanced by the provision of appropriately sized desks and chairs or their use of an alternate, less demanding position.)

83. Zack E, Barr R, Gerhardstein P, Dickerson K, Meltzoff AN (2009). Infant imitation from television using novel touch screen technology. *Br J Dev Psychol*; Mar;27 (Pt1):13-26

(This study looked at 15 month old children and their transfer of learning. They either used a real button to push for 3D or a virtual button on a screen for 2D. They were then given opportunities for cross-dimension conditions such as watching a demonstration of pushing the button in 3D and given the opportunity to reproduce the action in 2D or vice versa. Infants produced fewer target actions in the cross-dimension conditions than in the within-dimension conditions.)

Chapter 22

Special Needs Children

84. Fedrizzi E, Pagliano E, Marzaroli M, Fazzi E, Maraucci I, Furlanetto AR, Facchin P (2000). Developmental sequence of postural control in prone position in children with spastic diplegia. *Brain Dev*; 22(7):436-44

(A study of 24 children with a diagnosis of spastic diplegia and triplegia was done to study postural control in the prone position. Findings included that the acquisition of the full uprighting sequence in the prone position before the age of two related to the later acquisition of autonomous sitting.)

85. Fedrizzi E, Facchin P, Marzaroli M, Pagliano E, Botteon G, Percivalle L, Fazzi E (2000). Predictors of independent walking in children with spastic diplegia. *JChild Neurol*; (Ability to put weight on the hands while prone and to roll from supine to prone by 18 months was significantly related to independent walking while ability to sit without support was predictive only at around 24 months.)

86. Feldman R, Eidelman AI, Sirota L, Weller A (2002). Comparison of skin-to-skin (Kangaroo) and Traditional Care: Parenting Outcomes and Preterm Infant Development. *Pediatr*: 110:16-26
(This study was done on 146 preterm infants, 73 receiving kangaroo care [skin-to-skin contact with the parent] and 73 receiving more traditional care. The conclusion was that kangaroo care had a significant positive impact on the infant's perceptual-cognitive and motor development and on the parenting process.)

87. Fetters L, Huang HH (2007). Motor development and sleep, play, and feeding positions in very-low-birthweight infants with and without white matter disease. *Dev Med Child Neurol*; Nov; 49(11):804
(Prone position is important for development.)

88. Grandin, T (1992). Calming effects of deep touch pressure in patients with autistic disorder, college students, and animals. *JChild Adolesc Psychopharmacol*; Spring:2(1):63-72
(Temple Grandin's "squeeze machine" is discussed. A review of the literature shows that deep touch pressure is therapeutically beneficial for both children with autistic disorder and probably children with attention-deficit hyperactivity disorder.)

89. Otamiri G, Berg G, Ledin T, Leijon I, Lagercrantz H.(1991). Delayed neurological adaptation in infants delivered by elective cesarean section and the relation to catecholamine levels. *Early Hum Dev*; Jul;26(1):51-60 ("Statistically significant correlations were found between low CA[catecholamine] levels and poor muscle tone and/ or lower grade of excitability in the CS [cesarean section] infants.")

90. Schilling DL, Washington K, Billingsley FF, Deitz J. (2003). Classroom seating for children with attention deficit hyperactivity disorder: therapy balls versus chairs. *Am J Occup Ther*; Sep-Oct;57(5):534-41 (This single subject study was done with a 4th grade student. It showed that the use of therapy balls for seating in the classroom may facilitate in-seat behavior and legible word productivity.)

91. Turkewitz G, Kenny PA (1985). The role of developmental limitations of sensory input on sensory/perceptual organization. *J Dev Behav Pediatr*; 6:302-306. (Providing too much or the wrong stimulation can be harmful for premature infants. It is important to use a cautious approach in augmenting the stimulation of premature infants.)

Chapter 23

Adoption and Bonding Issues

92. Montagu A (1986). *Touching: The Human Significance of the Skin*, 3rd Ed. N. Y. Harper and Row Publishers. ("The infant will develop a sense of trust or mistrust depending upon his sensory impressions, received mainly through the skin, whether gratifying or not." [Pg 250-251] ". . . all babies will establish "eye contact" with their mothers

very quickly. This is important for the bonding which will take place between them."[Pg 264])

93. Murphy N.(2009), Facilitating attachment after international adoption. *Am J Matern Child Nurs*; Jul-Aug; 34(4):210-5
(In regards to treating attachment disorder . . . "Nurturing, highly responsive parenting requires parents to maintain near constant physical contact [preferably by carrying the child in a sling on the chest of the parent to promote, but not force eye contact], encouraging skin-to-skin contact, sleeping in close proximity, and nurturing the child with food and sucking [infant bottles are encouraged long past the usual age of weaning] [Gribble, 2007]. "Kangaroo holding" is another excellent intervention that promotes human touch to facilitate attachment (Johnson, 2005).")

About the Author

Roxanne Small is a registered physical therapist with over 35 years of experience in pediatrics. Her career has included working in hospitals, schools, homes, and clinics. Roxanne teaches a course in "Developmental Environments" to health care professionals working in the field of early intervention. She and her teaching partner, Julie Erbaugh, PT also teach professional seminars regarding Chronologically Controlled Developmental Therapy. In addition, Roxanne has been a guest speaker at conventions and meetings, speaking on topics relating to sensory-motor foundations in children. The first edition of *Building Babies Better* was published in 2005. Roxanne has more than 25 years of first-hand experience as a parent. Roxanne and her husband, Gary, have three children, all of whom have been the motivation and impetus for *Building Babies Better*.

Made in the USA
Lexington, KY
16 May 2018